10
GOLDEN
Steps of Life

10
GOLDEN
Steps of Life

VIKRMN:

Srishti
Publishers & Distributors

SRISHTI PUBLISHERS & DISTRIBUTORS
Registered Office: N-16, C.R. Park
New Delhi – 110 019
Corporate Office: 212A, Peacock Lane
Shahpur Jat, New Delhi – 110 049
editorial@srishtipublishers.com

First published by
Srishti Publishers & Distributors in 2016

Dedicated to my inspiration
Late Dr. A.P.J. Abdul Kalam sir.

Acknowledgements

❧

I am thankful to…

My family, for their love and support.

Friends, for being my partners in crime in all those getaways that unblocked the writer's block.

My readers, all my precious unknown friends out there who share my quotes and writing.

Colleagues, for providing that daily inspiration that gets scribbled in my notebook and enriches my writing.

CA fraternity, for reinforcing the values of the professionalism and perfectionism I strive to achieve.

My infatuations, for I work harder to impress them, so I set high standards for myself.

Those infatuated with me, precious few who make me smile that little extra and fill me with confidence.

People who like me in spite of my silliness, you deserve a mention just for putting up with me.

People who don't like me or my work, for they challenge me to perform better than before.

And last but not the least, team Srishti Publishers, for not just their seamless management and invaluable expertise, but also the art of making dreams come true.

If you wish to know more about me, please do write to me at v@vikrmn.com.

Contents

1

They are the victorious...
who dare not to give-up

❧

Quit giving up.

❖

Y*ou face failure, not the moment you are defeated, but the moment you give up fighting.*

Giving up is so easy, because it requires no efforts, just reasons and excuses for not pursuing something whole-heartedly and willingly.

If you make a mistake, it's ok. At least you tried.

Don't blame yourself for the failures, for it hampers your chances to improve, in turn also coaxing you to give up. Don't let it be your hobby.

Cultivate a "can-do" attitude in you, and top it up with the cherry of "won't-give-up"; victory would be certainly yours. Continuous self-criticism is rewarded with nothing but blood pressure problems.

Fall a thousand times; get up a thousand and one.

Here is a motivational story of a boy who changed the biggest failure of his life into the first greatest success of his life.

❖

There was once a studious boy, who was hard working and always excelled in studies. His name was Vin and he was studying for the last leg of his CA exam.

The day results were about to be declared, he was quite nervous. But he also had a sense of happiness within him. He had excelled in all exams till now, and was pretty confident that he'd make through. He and his friends had been anticipating the results around noon.

But when the results were out, it was still pretty early in the day and he was asleep. One of his friends called him up and asked for his roll number. He gave the details, but his friend didn't reply.

"What happened," Vin asked, now somewhat curious.

"Bro, are you sure this is your roll number?" his friend asked.

This was a terrifying question, especially on the day of the result. He gathered his voice firmly and replied, "Obviously! Don't you dare play any pranks with me right now. I'll kill you." He joked, thinking that his friend was up to some mischief.

"Why would I? I am serious," said the friend. "I am sorry, but your marks are less than the passing percentage."

"What!?" Vin shouted over phone. How could that be possible! He had always scored a distinction, and now someone was telling him he had failed in the final leg of his course. He had faltered on the very last step of his life as a student.

He steadied himself a little and asked, "Which subject did I score the lowest?"

"MICS," was all that he heard before going blank.

Vin was helpless, for the negativity had barged in. He could do nothing but study again and re-appear in the exams which were scheduled to be held in the next four months.

He had to go through that pain of studying the same subjects all over again, especially his favourite one due to which he had failed. There was no option he could get the answer sheet of the previous attempt to check where he had gone wrong.

Week by week, along with the studies, he was getting depressed. The way to channelize the anger seemed lost amidst the jungle of irritation.

Just two months later, Vin was at a press conference with his friend. It was after a long time that he was seen smiling. He felt the change in himself.

As the reporters gathered, everyone settled and the press conference started.

❖

Flashback: *One month before the press conference.*

Vin was browsing for something. When he got it, he picked up his mobile and dialled up the number he had found on the website.

The desk phone rang on the other side, buried under a whole lot of files and dozens of books.

It was a miracle the elderly man could hear it ringing under such weight.

"Hello," he said, still lost in the papers he was going through.

"Hi!" Vin asked hesitatingly. "Could I please talk to Mr. Sam?"

"May I know who's calling," the gentleman asked in return.

"My name is Vin and I need to speak to him regarding a book," he said.

"Ok, please wait a moment while I connect you to him," said the old man without much ado. He put Vin's call on hold and transferred the call to his boss.

"Hello, Sam here," replied a deep baritone voice.

"Hi Mr. Sam! Vin here."

"Do we know each other, Vin?" Sam asked, not recalling anyone by that name.

"No sir, but I am sure you can help me," Vin said politely and firmly. He knew he had to do this.

"How can I help you?" Sam wanted to come straight to the point.

"I want to talk to you regarding a book."

"Oh, which book?" asked Sam, picking up a book out of the many on his table, flipping through the pages to check the print. A triangular copper plate shone bright out of the pages and books that clouded everything else on the desk. It read – EDITOR-IN-CHIEF.

"MICS," Vin replied.

"Hmm, what does it stand for?" Sam asked, still engrossed in the book in his hands. He was a man with much reading to do and he believed in making every second count.

"Management Information and Control Systems."

"Information Technology?"

"Yes sir," Vin said, hopeful that he will now have Sam's full attention.

"So do you want to buy it or sell it? I mean, are you a dealer or a supplier?"

"None, sir. I want to get it published under your publishing house's banner."

"Oh, like that! That's good to hear. May I know who the author is?"

"I am the author, sir," Vin said humbly.

"Oh great!" The editor raised his brows along with the pitch of his voice. Excitement perhaps, Vin thought. "For which syllabus can it be used?" he further asked Vin.

"The subject falls under CA."

"Those books do very well. That means you are a CA, right?" quipped the editor.

"Umm, not really."

"Oh, may be an IT professional?"

"No sir," Vin replied.

The editor was surprised and couldn't take any more guesses. "Then?"

"I am a student."

"What?! A student?"

"Yes sir."

"Of?"

"CA final year," Vin said softly.

"Are you taking me for a ride, kid? Because if you are…it's not funny." There was silence for a moment and Sam continued, "Is this book for CA Foundation or Intermediate level?"

"No sir," the guy replied with confidence, "This book is for final year students."

Now, there was silence. Absolute, pin-drop silence on both sides. After about half-a-minute, Vin checked if Sam was still on the line.

"Hello…Hello?"

Vin took the phone off his ear and checked the phone screen. The call was still connected as the timer was running.

"Hello, sir? Are you there?"

"Umm, yeah!" Sam broke his silence.

"So…," Sam spoke after a pause, "Sorry I forgot your name."

"It's Vin, sir!"

"Yes! *Sir* Vin!" the editor smiled at his sarcasm and said, "So, you have cleared your second group of CA final year that includes this subject, I presume."

"Well..." Vin faltered for just a second, but Sam interfered before he could complete.

"How much did you say you scored in MICS?"

"You see..." Vin tried to speak again, but couldn't gather enough courage. He knew it was a crucial piece of information for Sam and he didn't have anything to say.

Sam asked, without waiting for his reply, "And why do you think students will read your book?"

Vin was quiet. Thinking of how to put it.

"*Sir* Vin!" the editor probed. "Would you please tell me why?"

"I..." Vin replied with a pause, "I haven't..."

"Haven't what?" Sam was getting impatient now.

"I haven't cleared any groups in the CA final year, sir."

"Oh!" the editor paused, perhaps out of shock.

"Hello...Sir?" Vin checked, almost sure that Sam had disconnected the call this time.

"Yes *sir,*" Sam replied mimicking the guy, "Carry on...*sir!*"

"I..." Vin fumbled, "I...did appear for the exams...but..."

"But?"

"But I..."

"Ahem."

"I failed."

"What?" He was shocked.

"Yes sir."

"Aww!" Sam sympathised, but Vin couldn't guess whether this was genuine or he was being sarcastic again. "You failed in group one of CA final year?"

"It so happened..." Vin was trying to frame a sensible reply, but Sam couldn't wait.

"You got an exemption in group two for MICS paper then, I think."

"No sir! I failed in group two actually..." Vin paused to gather courage to speak. The last bit could really end this conversation.

"And?" Sam was either trying to help the guy be comfortable or he was making him more nervous.

"...and I failed due to this particular paper," he finally said it out loud.

"What? You failed MICS?" the editor was on his toes.

Vin had a lump in his throat when he said, "Yes, sir. And I got.. twenty-eight marks."

The volume and pitch at which Sam said "What?" this time was a new record even for him. It was way less than passing marks, i.e. forty.

Sam had shouted out so loud that the old assistant who had first taken the call came to his cabin, almost running. "Sir?" asked the assistant, "What happened sir? Is everything alright?"

"Oh, yes *sir!*" Sam mimicked Vin while replying to the assistant.

"Do you need any kind of help, sir?" the assistant asked again.

"No sir!" the editor said, but quickly added, after perhaps an afterthought.

"Wait wait," the editor waved at him just when he was leaving, "Come-in, sit and listen to this guy."

Sam turned on the speaker of his desk phone and said, "Sir Vin, I have my assistant with me in my cabin. If that's not a problem with you, could you please continue?"

"Sure sir!" Vin replied, his ears red hot out of sheer anxiety and nervousness.

"So you were telling me about your MICS score," he prompted Vin.

"Twenty-eight marks, sir."

"Sorry to hear that, but what surprises me is," Sam laughed and cried making faces to the assistant, "It's kind of wonderful that you want us to publish your book!"

"Yes sir," the guy sensed Sam's mockery.

In the meantime, Sam turned to his assistant and whispered with hands on his head, "What type of calls do you keep transferring to me?"

"Sorry sir," Vin said, having heard Sam talk to his assistant.

"Sorry Sir Vin!" the editor quipped, "I was asking why do you think students will read your book?"

"I am sure they'll read this book, sir."

"I am asking why, sir. Tell me why!" his voice bounced back.

Vin heaved a deep sigh and said, "I would have cut my veins after the result. I was shocked to know that I have failed due to a very bad score in my favourite subject, MICS. My world came crashing down. Where people had expected me to score a distinction, because I had always topped till then, I had failed. That too due to low marks in my favourite subject, MICS. I had taught that subject to my friends, and they all got good marks."

He took a moment's break before continuing, "It was a shocking moment for my family as well; they had great expectations from me. After all, I had never failed in any exam before this."

"Listen, Vin, I am sorry you had to go through this, but you have to understand my position too," Sam said.

"Absolutely sir. I have lived through the negativity that encumbered my thoughts. While my friends, family members and acquaintances have all sympathised with me, you aren't the first stranger who is mocking me."

Sam was looking at his assistant who indicated him something with a smile.

"And honestly, all I wanted was to see my answer sheet, so as to know why I failed. Unfortunately, it was against the institution's policies. So out of frustration, I thought about filing a suit to get my answer sheet. My peers and friends suggested me not to take that route as I would be disqualified by the institute. The rage and anger burning inside me was immeasurable. But my parents taught me one thing…"

"Give-up the giving-up."

"So I thought not to give up. I decided to do something. And converted my notes into a 319-pages-long book. I have cracked the ways to understand MICS and I have named it *MICS Unleashed*."

"Sir Vin!" Sam replied smiling, "I can understand all that, but we are not doing business for taking chances."

"Sir!" Vin replied promptly. "I got good marks in IT subjects at other levels of CA, and I was expecting 82 in CA Final, but got 28."

Vin's voice had now gained the confidence that was needed. But silence spilled over.

This time, Vin didn't check if Sam had disconnected the call or not.

"Sir!" Vin continued, "People fluke pass exams; I fluke failed. And that too due to my favourite subject."

Sam was quiet, but Vin was not. He said, "I might get rejected by your publishing house because of a few criteria, or from other publishers too for many other reasons, but I will not give up. I will continue my struggle. For me, MICS is always the question – 'Am I continuing the struggle?' And my answer is a big YES."

"Hmm." Sam smiled followed by the assistant.

Vin continued, "I don't know what went wrong, but I know how to make it right…I have *the key* that students would want to crack MICS.'

"But," Sam asked, "Do you think students will prefer your book over those by other established authors?"

"Yes sir!" Vin replied confidently. "They'll read it for the new things I have introduced."

"New things? Like what?" Sam seemed bit interested.

"Like a chapter map summarising an entire chapter in just one page, 'Double Trouble' to resolve the confusing questions, memorising links to avoid cramming, Abbreviation Bank, simplest graphs and figures and a bonus too."

"Oh! What Bonus?" Sam was curious.

"I'll price it at half the other books. That way, no student would have to think twice before buying it. Like they do now for the other costly CA books."

"That's Interesting." Sam laughed lightly and quipped, "But that'll decrease your royalty!"

"I am not doing this for money, sir. I am doing this for my own satisfaction and my parents' happiness."

"Okay!" Sam raised his brows looking at the assistant who replied with a smile and asked, "But do you think I'll publish it?"

"Sir, you're speaking to a boy who hasn't learnt to give up, be it failure in exams or failure in life. Rather than cribbing or crying, I chose this way, and I am sure the book will find someone for itself on its own."

"Nice."

Vin added, "And I contacted you thinking you'll be the best judge for this IT book, because you yourself are an IT Auditor."

"Ha ha." Sam smirked, "IT is my favourite subject too, and that's why I am still listening to you. Otherwise I would have disconnected this call long back."

"Now that you're slightly interested, like you just said, please also let me know when you'd like to have a look at the sample chapters?" Vin said politely.

Sam patted the assistant's shoulder and spoke into the phone, "Young man, I like your confidence!"

Sam then asked the assistant, "Sir, what do you say?"

"submissions@itbooks.com," replied the assistant with a smile.

"God!" Sam said, breaking into a light laughter this time, "Everyone is to the point, brilliantly intelligent and even filmy these days."

"Sir, I have noted down the mail ID," Vin prompted.

"Perfect Sir Vin," Sam replied. "Send us the sample chapters and we'll get back to you in a week's time."

"Sure sir! Thank you so much!"

"Actually I should say thanks to you," Sam replied. "I had till now only heard about a particular type of people who never give up, no matter what life throws at them. It felt good to see that they exist. Good luck, son. Keep it up!"

❖

Thus, to turn the anger in him into positive energy, he decided to vent out the fumes by authoring a book on the same subject he had failed in.

The press conference was nothing but the launch of the book *MICS Unleashed*, while he was still studying the same subject. His story was covered by seven newspapers on the very front page, and even on a few TV channels.

He cleared his exam in the next attempt with flying colours. The book sold like hot cakes for almost two years, until the syllabus was changed by the institute.

Had he quit after the failure and not channelized the negative energy into positive, he wouldn't have tasted the first greatest success of his life. Which brings us to a very important anecdote:

Quit thinking negative.

❖

So here is a rule to be followed when failure knocks at your door, especially before the arrival of an opportunity:

Open the door, kick the failure out, lock the door from outside and go in search of the opportunity that you had till now been waiting for. Don't sit back. Don't wait.

If you fail, it's fine. Sow another idea or refine the same one; irrigate it with perseverance and cultivate it with the manure of faith. The harvest would be the fruit of success.

The most important ingredient for the recipe of success is patience, with a little bit of perseverance sprinkled to taste.

We often ignore that there is a third dimension also, beyond success and failure. It is neutrality, which means getting no results; neither negative nor positive, just a zero.

In case you come across any of these three dimensions, people might laugh at you, come and advise you about things that you have known better than them all your life. Let it be.

Someday you are the guitarist; someday you are the guitar.

You can't control people's perception about you. So let them fly on their thoughts; you soar high and give yourself another chance and your ideas another try.

But even if the decision to quit is in consideration, then check again at which stage your efforts are. Never quit when the results are neutral, because in that case, more efforts and means can be realised to reach the goal. If the decision to quit is taken because of negativity of results or failure, just ask yourself the following question:

"Can I sleep with the regret that I couldn't do it?"

If the answer is a *yes*, then it's not your dream project. Just wrap it up and move on. Believe me, if the act in question means anything to you, anything at all, the answer would never be a yes. Because no one would want to sleep daily with regret.

If the answer is a *no*, but you still think you can't do it, then *quit*. It would mean that you don't have it in you to cross these hurdles. So just *Cry. Sleep. Repeat.*

I am sure nobody would want to follow the above rule. So the only way to get away from it is to do something about it.

The problem arises when there's a dilemma. But again, it's simple. You are right in two cases:

If you think you can't do it, you are right. If you think you can do it, you are right.

It's never in the world outside that lies the inspiration and will to finish a task; it lies within. So if you just think that you *can do it* and if it is your dream, no one in the world can tell you that you can't, not even you yourself. So don't ask, just DO IT.

When the wind is against you, be like a kite; have your chord of faith rooted and you would fly higher than ever.

If the reason to quit is that someone has stolen your idea and you don't feel like taking it ahead anymore, then remember...

Those who love doing things without bothering for credits are the real winners. They don't care about one or two golden eggs that people steal, for they have the factory.

If you wish to quit because you think you cannot cope with the stress of daily challenges of your personal life, then think again.

Ebbs and flows are a part of life, and they remind you who you are, where you have come from and where you can go.

And if you want to quit because you failed then...

Learn to lose, wade to win. If you win, people will quote your examples; if you lose, you can guide others on how not to paddle.

It's best to learn from your failures, and that cannot hold true if you quit. Anyway, a goal with surety of success happens only in the imaginary world.

The ladder of success is made from nails of patience.

Every success story has a struggle attached to it. That's the only flavour of success.

Success is like an umbrella. It has wires of faith holding it together. It has no meaning if there is no rain.

*P.S.: Never get confused between quitting and giving up.
Quitting is giving something up; giving up is quitting everything.

2

Quit the rat race...
to lead your own.

❦

Take a break,
for you are not made
to win this rat race.
Try something different,
something unique;
something worth failing,
worth falling.

❖

Before we move forth to the rat race that binds so many of us in our everyday lives, let's talk a bit about the awesome and great thing called life. More specifically, your work life.

Let's begin with just one simple question, rather than pouring so many fancy ones. "Are you really happy at work as far as your dreams are concerned? Are you enjoying yourself?"

In eighty percent of the cases, the answer is *no*. Hardly anyone says that my work is my hobby. Most of the people don't even know whether they are living their dream work-life or not.

In any of the above cases, all that is required is to just pause, take out some time and think, "Am I just another rat in the race?"

You don't need to be. You are unique. Be different. You were not born to be a part of the herd. If you think that your work-life has become monotonous, then take a break. Take time to rethink and redefine your goals. In case you find yourself stuck in the vicious circle of unproductive and aimless work-life, you need to take a step, the remedial step. This step would make a drastic change in your approach to innovation or your problem solving attitude.

Challenge yourself by asking yourself whether you are pursuing your ambitions or not, whether you are leading the work-life that you had actually imagined and dreamt of for yourself or not.

Being different is the same as being same.

You don't always need to do what others are doing, unless and until your high-pay-pack job demands so. By this we don't mean that you leave your current job or profession that is giving you exposure to this world and obviously helping you pay your bills and EMI.

Just stop telling yourself that since the world works this way, so do you.

You can lie to all but one, yourself.

Be different from the herd. Don't burn your brain just for the sake of working or showing that you are working. Instead of taking extreme steps, you can innovate in your current work area. For this you need to experiment and take a few risks. On that path, you might fail, you might get competition or criticism, but you have to keep going.

One of the most mistaken corporate rules is survival of the fittest "spoon", the one who is obsequious. Those who follow it, reach nowhere.

❖

Don't do anything just because everyone else is doing it. The following story would make this statement clearer.

Neil was young, and brilliant at academics. He was famous among his peers, classmates, neighbourhood and even colleagues for his innovative and out of the box thinking. He had studied very hard for five long years to become the efficient professional that he was well-known as.

Just when he had finished his studies, with big dreams in his eyes, he was very enthusiastic for his first interview call which was scheduled with one of the largest and most high profile IT companies.

Soon after, he got a call that having cleared the initial round of interviews, he was invited for a face to face round at the nearest location. It was scheduled after two days.

He reached the interview venue a little before time on the scheduled day. As he entered the room, he saw a panel of three interviewers to greet him. He had a firm handshake with all of them and took his seat.

The interview started with his introduction, followed by his studies and training related experiences. Once the technical round was over, the interviewers came to a few selected questions to judge his stability as a candidate.

"Where do you see yourself five years from now?" asked one of the interviewers.

"Well, on your chair," he said confidently, looking in the eyes of the interviewer. "I'll be interviewing candidates."

"Good one," laughed the interviewer, who was a senior manager and added, "Young man! It took me ten years to reach here."

"I might take five or ten or maybe fifteen years," the boy said, "but I promise to give it my best shot."

He was not selected, for reasons that can be obviously guessed.

Now, three years later, Neil was working at another company. In these three years, he had learnt many things about the corporate world.

He had realised that everyone was running in a rat race. Everyone was after promotions. Not just to outshine others, but to create a cut-throat competition as well. And the management only encouraged it, because with the employees' heightened efforts and internal competition, their work quality and output also improved.

But the inner reality was that only a few people actually wanted to work; rest everyone wanted to take credit for the other person's work. Due to the pressure to outshine others, suppressing others with office politics became the core agenda at work, pushing back healthy competition of any sort. In a way, no one wanted to genuinely appreciate good work done by others.

Neil found himself stuck in that rat race. His creativity and innovation was nowhere recognised in that world. Despite his great performance at work and appreciation mails from clients, he was struggling for his promotion as a Manager. All the reasons management gave him was the fancy "bell-curve theory" and plans of some non-existent bigger and wider roles for him in the pipeline which hadn't materialised in the last two years.

At last, getting fed up with it, he decided to switch his job and uploaded his profile on various job search websites. His profile was shortlisted by one of the telecom giants and the interview was scheduled.

He steered through the preliminary rounds easily. He was gearing up for the technical round sitting in front of the management panel of three. The job and work related discussion went well and they started with questions on general experience.

"What value-add would you give to the company?" asked the old man, one of the three interviewers.

"I had implemented twenty-one innovative ideas in my previous company that resulted in process improvement and big cost saving for the company. I would bring in the same zeal and ideas to this company as well."

"Oh, good! But I guess you would make people unemployed," smirked another one.

"Nope," he replied, "I helped my team to go home early by finishing their work with automated processes in lesser time rather than their burning midnight oil in the manual process."

"Good good," the interviewer laughed adding, "But that's what we pay them for, working long hours."

"I think," he replied humbly, "a team should stay back only if there is unavoidable work. Once it's done, leaving in time is the best thing to do."

"We want *them* to be hardworking, we want *them* to be more productive, we want *them* to add value to the company... more revenue should be generated if they have time to spare. We want *them* to be multi-taskers."

"*Them* who, sir, if I may ask?" Neil quipped.

"The employees obviously."

"Oh, sorry. I had had a habit of addressing *them* as a team so I couldn't understand you."

The interviewer smirked pointing a pen towards him, "See! When you become a manager, you are above *them*; you have to be the people's manager."

"I believe in being a good leader; becoming a manager, AVP or a VP is all about designations. These are aspirations, but not the final goals."

"Very well said," he laughed looking at others and added, "We won't make you a manager then. Ha ha ha." Now all three of them laughed and he looked at them.

"Anyway, where do you see yourself after five years?" asked one controlling his laughter.

"In some other company," he replied with confidence.

"What?" the interviewer was surprised.

"Because," he replied confidently, "I have different ideas and a different way of working that is not recognised by my current company. That's why I am here, in this interview, searching for another job. And I suspect that if the same would happen again in three years, I'll be looking out for another company."

The panel of interviewers looked at each other.

"I apologise if my answer is disrespectful to your organisation in any way," he said, "but I want to be true from my heart. I don't want to please you guys with my fancy answers and then later not feel contended with my job responsibilities."

Another three years passed by.

He was contended at the work front as his out of the box thinking and innovative ideas were well received and recognised in the company. There came a big corporate event where industry leaders were invited to share their ideas that changed the way of working in the industry and proved a boon for the rapidly growing customer driven market. The event was attended by a thousand plus participants where three to four companies were selected and awarded for their leadership ideas and out of the box thoughts.

Neil was there to attend the event too. He settled on a table with his colleagues and started sipping coffee, cracking jokes. A gentleman approached him and patted his shoulder.

"Young man! How are you?"

He turned back holding the glass in his hand. "Oh! Mr. Ron, hi!" Neil got up immediately, grabbing his hand. "What a pleasant surprise!"

"Oh, you remember my name?" the gentleman asked.

He was the same old man who had interviewed him in the past.

"Yes sir," he replied. "I am good at remembering names."

He smiled and said, "Hah, I just forgot yours, ha ha ha."

He smiled and then turned to his colleagues and introduced him, "Hey friends! This is Mr. Ron, CEO of one of the top finance agencies... a brilliant person and a great leader."

Everyone greeted him while he looked surprised.

"You know that I got promoted as CEO?" Mr. Ron replied raising his head a bit.

"Yes sir! The industry news travels fast, you know."

He nodded and asked warmly, "So, young man, how is it going now? I hope you are happy with your professional aspirations?"

"Yes sir," he said and smiled. "Sort of."

Ron nodded but said patting Neil's shoulder, "But young man, your answer looses that confidence today. I liked your confidence that day in your interview with us, especially the answer that you gave me."

"Oh, you remember?"

"Yes, I do," the CEO replied. "I always give an example of your confidence to *them* in my leadership meets in the company."

"*Them* who?" the young man asked innocently.

"Our employees," said the old man pointing to his team and walked him to them.

"You know, we got sixty seats booked for our employees for this event," he continued with pride. "We are attending this from the past so many years. We want our employees to imbibe all the innovative ideas that are shared and discussed here. Very few are fortunate to attend such events, young man. Welcome to the party."

"Oh, I see!" he said looking at his team holding diaries, pens and laptops in their hands and waved at them.

Then he saw two more people in the group. They were the same two interviewers in the panel that day who had sat next to Ron. They were whispering something between themselves as they saw him and smiled.

He smiled back waving at them but noticed the next moment that almost everyone was whispering and faking a smile at him.

He looked at the CEO in surprise.

The CEO said, "They have always heard about you from me. Today they are seeing you for the first time, so they are very happy."

He was still looking at the CEO, straight into his eyes. He understood that the story Ron might have told them about his replies in the interview to be the silliest ever.

"Ladies and gentlemen!" announced a lady from stage, "A very warm welcome to this event of ideas and innovations award ceremony."

Ron patted his shoulder and took him aside, "See! Don't worry, they don't know your name. But you need to learn the corporate culture and that's how you go up the success ladder."

Neil nodded, "Hmm."

"By the way, what's your name?" Ron asked.

Just when the young man was about to reply, the anchor announced on stage, "Please put your hands together for our first speaker of the day."

"Oh, the conference has started. We'll catch up later," said Ron, rushing towards the stage.

"Sir, here's my card!" Neil said giving it to him.

"Thanks," the CEO took the card and slid it into his pocket. "See you later."

Neil stood there, looking and smiling at his team.

Ron went to his team, took the card out and gave it to his colleague who had been the co-interviewer that day.

"Good luck sir!" said a team member to Ron.

"Thank you!" Ron said looking at him, smiled with pride and then turned back to his team. "Be ready to jot down all the ideas. Give me a pen and notepad too." He took the notepad and went towards the stage.

"Let's welcome Mr...," said the lady from the dais and the hall erupted into loud applause.

Ron soon vanished in the crowd towards the stage, while Neil stood there, looking at his back. The co-interviewer looked at him, folded his visiting card, took out his pen, and tried writing on the back of the card to check if the pen was working and smiled.

Neil felt as if his face was being scratched with that pen, but he stood helpless. He looked back at Ron's team; a few of them were still looking at him and laughing.

Neil picked up his laptop. His own team looked at him but he was lost in thoughts and then went out.

The lady on the stage had taken over the microphone again and said, "The one to bag the Innovator of the Year title has titled his entry '5 ups of life'. Ladies and gentlemen, please give a round of applause for the innovator, and let's hear from the winner himself what these ups of life are."

The hall resonated with a huge round of applause. The CEO's team clapped out loud, to congratulate the winner. After all, it was his ideas that they were going to copy and implement.

"Dear friends..." said a vibrantly charged voice from the stage, the speaker standing in the middle of the stage with open arms, "Thank you for such a warm welcome."

Ron's team sat there under a spell, as if unable to stop clapping. In fact, one more person sitting next to the stage, in the front row, on one of the VIP seats, was also found staring at the speaker with eyes wide open in surprise.

Ron turned back looking at his team with surprise and found his team as stunned as he himself was.

The person standing on stage was none other than Neil.

Ron quickly reached out for the visiting card in his pocket, but found none. He again looked back at his team members who were still clapping in slow motion, as if in a trance. As Ron looked at them in anger, they stopped clapping.

Ron indicated at them to look for the young man's visiting card. The co-interviewer had thrown it off, and immediately bent under the table to pick up the card and unfolded it. He nodded to the CEO confirming the young man's name embossed on the card, which had been announced a few moments back.

Ron turned his face back to the stage and passed a fake smile before holding his head. Just then, a guy patted oh his shoulder. He turned his head around to see one of his team members standing there.

"What?" Ron asked holding back his anger.

"Sir!" he said unfolding the visiting card and gave it to him, "You wanted this back?"

The CEO looked at him with an almost blank face which had now lost colour.

"Sorry sir!" the chap said realising that Ron was angry. "I thought you asked for the card," and he ran back to his seat.

Ron looked at the card that read the young man's designation: "Senior Manager."

His mobile phone tinkled with an SMS. It was from the co-interviewer. "Sir, no worries. I am sure we will get a chance to go on stage the next year and represent our company." Ron could just swallow his anger at that time. He didn't want his team laughing at him, and that's exactly what this was going to end up in.

"Oh, this is the chap?" said another CEO sitting next to him, pulling the card from his hand and added, "Brilliant guy, such a great achievement at this age."

Ron had no option but to nod with a smile.

"A warm welcome to all of you," said the young man from the stage, holding the microphone.

"*5 ups of life: Buckle up, Start up, Keep it up, Don't give up, Cheer up.*"

He went on for a few minutes while the listeners heard him out with bated breath. He had been fabulous. The moment he completed, the hall resonated with applause.

Ron's team clapped the hardest; perhaps they could see their dream in Neil's achievement.

Neil went on to share his ideas that his company had implemented and had got a great response in the market. "I wish you all great luck in the professional world ahead." He concluded after the question and answer session.

"Any messages for the young guns?" asked the moderating lady.

"Yup, one thing..." he nodded and continued,

"*Always give your best. It doesn't always mean you would get back the best. But that doesn't mean you give up giving your best.*"

The listeners broke into a loud cheer this time.

"*Be different,*" he continued, "*Trying something different won't ensure that you would be liked by everyone. But still... Go on...*"

There was a deafening round of applause now.

"I was never satisfied with my own work and aspired to do it better, every time I did it. And today, I am here, sharing the ideas that our team has nourished. Please give them a big hand," he said pointing to his table. "Guys! Come up here. It would not have been possible without you."

Everyone looked back, towards the team and they all quickly headed towards the stage.

Neil continued, "Be innovative, do it differently, don't follow the rate race. If you don't like it the way it is and you think that you have a better way, then implement it. If you are prevented from implementing it, find a better company, or start your own business."

Some people on the VIP seats even gave him a standing ovation, followed by many others in the audience.

Ron raised his brows while clapping forcefully and was in shock as his team also stood in honour; some of them still looking at him with hope in their eyes.

In the next hour, the other three winning ideas were also shared and the moment came for the award ceremony.

The head of the industrial chamber was invited on stage to felicitate the achievers. After the ceremony, the Director of the company shared a few words on stage.

"We asked this young man in the interview, where do you see yourself after five years? And his reply won our hearts."

Everyone seemed curious to know his answer while Neil looked at Ron shirking eyes. The words echoed in his ears, "You'll find me in another company if I don't get space for my out of the box thinking here."

There were soft murmurs as everyone was surprised at Neil's confidence in himself and firm faith.

"Would you like to share a final message for everyone out here?" asked the gorgeous lady anchor.

"Yup!" he smiled adding, "If you want to stop something, then stop pleasing everyone. If you want to quit, then quit one thing.

"*Quit the rat race, to lead your own.*"

❖

To quit the rat race, all you need to do is,

"*Quit being change-phobic.*"

If the roads to your dreams are not there already, dreams would make them. People who just sit and watch won't see even the existing paths.

It's absolutely fine to be working to earn money, and that would need you to be in the rat race. Do it, but only for as long as it's necessary. Because once you get caught in the habit of a sub-standard living, you will forget to live your dreams.

Excess of everything is bad.

Don't play with your career and aspirations. The expectations you had of yourself as a youngster should not be run over by the monotony of this mechanical professional existence.

Coal mines, like a hard life, have seen the best diamonds of innovation, more than any jewel factory.

❖

P.S.: The rule "Never Quit" stated in a separate chapter is not applicable if it's a rat race.

3

Own your way...
your own way.

Sometimes
life is like a vacuum cleaner.
you know what it does.
all you need to do is
kick the power plug,
take the charge and...
Define your Destiny.

Never give the charge of your life in the hands of others; you'll get screwed and people would enjoy it. Life is like a guitar. So hold the guitar of your destiny, and play it well. Don't depend on others. If you believe in something, do it.

But for that, it is most essential to first believe in yourself. If you won't, then there's no way that the others would believe in you. You have to listen to your heart and then walk on the path it guides you to.

Drive, or get driven by change.

Even if circumstances are not fair to you, keep going, without losing the charge of your path that leads you to your goals.

Don't just be yourself, evolve yourself.

The worst mistake that most of us make is to misjudge whose happiness holds priority in our life. Don't change yourself to make the world happy; bring a change to be happy. People can advise, guide, taunt or even curse you for being you, but you have to work towards making yourself a better person and being happy. This won't apply to an infamous person indulging in non-ethical or wrong-doings.

If no one else can be you, then why to be someone else?

Retain your individuality, your way that you have chosen, not what others like you to be. And once you choose the path, stride non-stop.

A self-made struggling person is a lot better than the one living a fake life successfully.

Face the problems that run after you head on. Look at them in the eyes and be ready to quash them like a bull looks at the red colour. Take the hardships of life as challenges and use them positively to revamp your life. If problems are like rain, your will and positivity would be the sunshine. So...

If it rains during sunshine, don't worry; you'll see your rainbow.

Above all, this is your life and to lead it greatly, don't let others define or curtail your happiness.

❖

Here is a story of a girl named Myra who proved how "*You carve your own destiny.*"

"Mom, I have got the train ticket booked," said Myra while packing her bags. She was preparing for the next day to go to her native village where a religious ceremony was to be held.

"Okay baby," her mother said, "but please make sure you pack all the items I told you from the list which are to be offered in the *yajna*."

"Yes Mom. I have done that," she replied holding the mobile between her cheek and shoulder while pulling the chain of the travel bag.

"Leave in time for the train, ok?" her mother said. "Guru Ji advised me to tell you to travel safe, and this time, please don't miss the train like you did in December."

"Mom, you know it was not my mistake."

"I know baby, it was the train's fault to have left on time. You were running after the train to tell the driver that he should have waited for you."

"Mom, I am not coming."

"Ok, don't come."

"Mom?!" she said exasperated.

"What?" she replied lovingly.

"I had a huge bag on my back and I had to run past the bridge with it. That's why I missed the train."

"Alright, alright. Let's not talk about it now. But please leave half an hour early this time, ok?"

"Okay Mom. See you soon then, good night for now. And please wake me up early tomorrow so that I reach the station in time. Love yoooou."

"Love you honey. Good night," her mother said lovingly and hung up.

Next morning, she got up in time, thanks to her Mom. She got ready and was just having her breakfast when her mobile rang.

"Hi Mommy! I am ready. Gooood morning."

"Good morning sweetie! Have you booked the taxi?"

"It's still one hour, Mom. These days the taxis arrive in maximum ten minutes. I will book one soon."

"Myra! Book it NOW! Please!" her mother said lovingly, ensuring that nothing went wrong this time.

"Ok, I will make the booking in half an hour. Okay?"

"Done!"

When the taxi arrived some forty minutes later, she took her two bags full of stuff that the driver helped her in dragging to the taxi.

"I have a train to catch," she said to the driver, "Please make me reach as early as possible."

"Ok madam! Don't worry," said the driver with a smile.

On the way to the station, she was talking to a friend back home over phone, making plans to meet soon. They had hardly travelled for about ten minutes when she noticed that the speed of the taxi was slowly decreasing. The taxi came to a complete halt thereafter.

"Oh God!" the driver sighed.

"What happened?" Myra asked the driver.

"Madam, tyre puncture," he said peeping out to check which tyre it was.

"Oh God! How can it get punctured *now* of all times?"

"I don't know madam," he said locating the tyre and ran for the spare tyre from the boot of the car.

"Arrey! You should have driven carefully. I told you I have to reach the station in time. I am going for a very urgent visit to my home town," she told the driver in tension.

"Madam, what can I do? This is not in my control. I can only change the tyre."

That wasted a good thirty minutes of her precious time. She tried booking another cab, but none was available till the next fifteen minutes. She thought it'd be wise to wait for the guy to change the tyre. To kill her anxiety and control the frustration she was feeling, she called up back home. "Mom!" she said helplessly, "I will miss the train for sure."

Her mother was shocked as she explained the whole situation. But said positively, "I have full faith that you'll catch the train. I'll call Guru Ji."

"Oh Mumma please! What can Guru Ji do for a punctured tyre! If there's any person who can make me catch my train, it's this taxi driver. There is no other taxi nearby on this mobile app."

"Ok, no problem baby, calm down," the mother consoled her. "You don't need to get so worked up. It's fine. Do your best, and if it gets too late, just go back home and we will book a ticket for tomorrow."

Meanwhile, the taxi driver had changed the tyre, and they quickly left for the station. They reached the station just ten minutes before the departure time of the train.

The girl requested the taxi driver, "Can you please help me take the luggage to the platform?"

The challenge was that they had to cross a bridge to reach the platform of the station, and it would easily take at least ten minutes. So, the taxi guy refused politely. Moreover, he could not have left the taxi unattended in such a crowded place.

"Coolie!" The taxi guy shouted as he saw one and helped the girl to take the luggage out from the car.

The girl asked the coolie to run with one of her travel bags while she was carrying the stroller with the laptop. On the way to the platform, the coolie asked, "Madam, platform number?"

"Number one! Run, run, run! Don't stop!" said the girl pulling the stroller that she was holding.

As they reached the over-bridge of the station, the departure of the train was announced by the station master.

"Oh god, run faster please," said the girl. Escaping the crowd and pushing a few people, they somehow reached the escalator.

"Madam, train!" shouted the coolie pointing towards the train that had started moving.

They both ran towards the stairs. Even though the train was departing, Myra had decided to not leave her efforts midway. She will give it her best, she had told herself and her mother.

By the time they reached downstairs, the last wagon had passed in front of her. "Run, run!" she kept on yelling, following the train, even though she was short of breath. The coolie slowed down as the train continued to pick up speed. He was sure this train had gone.

"Leave it dear," said an elderly man standing on the platform. "Don't chase the train. Time and train wait for none." He chuckled looking at her.

She ignored it and asked the coolie to just keep running. She was shouting "Come on…run, run" and kept running towards the departing train.

"Oh God!" she suddenly yelled in shock.

The train had slow down a bit. The coolie rushed along with her, jaw dropped in amazement. He had never experienced a train slowing once it started off.

"Run…" she yelled with joy to the coolie.

Certain other people on the platform started cheering for her and yelled, "Run…Run."

Many people started taking pictures and recording the videos of that great event.

As she reached near the train, it had come to a complete halt. The person on the wagon stairs helped her to let her in.

She was short of breath but pulled up the bag from the coolie and quickly gave him a crisp note.

"Madam, no change," he said.

"Don't worry! Get chocolates for your children," she said, her hands still on her waist, her breath still not catching up.

It was no less than a movie. The determination of the girl to go her way, in her own way, had changed her destiny.

The person in the last wagon offered her his seat to relax on.

As she settled and took a few sips of water, she said to that person who seemed to be a railway official, "Thank you so much."

"You are welcome, take your time."

She just laughed and couldn't express her happiness.

A deep sigh escaped her and she asked him, "But I am surprised you stopped. Why did you do that?"

The official told her, "I saw you running. I was happy to see your determination to catch the train, so I stopped."

She fell short of words, but managed to utter a meek "Really?"

The railway official laughed a bit and said, "Not entirely. You see, the train had to wait at the station exit point for some time. So I thought why not here instead of there? It's the same thing…but this would give you some happiness too."

Her ear to ear smile warranted her happiness. She thanked him again, waited there for another ten minutes and walked on towards her compartment.

Had she not continued running for the train, even though it seemed like it had already left, she would not have been able to make it home for the religious festival.

Her faith that "*People make their own destiny,*" remained unshaken.

❖

Some people will discourage and mislead you in your path. If you fail, you'll be made fun of, and not just behind your back, but on your face too. These are those detractors that will tell you to give up whatever you are doing. Rather, some people would make you realise on your face that your decision was the worst decision ever.

You must ignore the naysayers and continue to believe in yourself.

A single day, good or bad, will not define your journey. You are defined by the never-give-up attitude that you carry at all times.

Choose your path wisely, the path of truthfulness. Have the courage to listen to your heart. Your mind would overpower your choices with practical problems. But if you have a strong gut feeling, go for it! Follow your way, your own way.

Life as a defeated warrior with dignity is a lot better than the king ruling without it.

Take your time to make the best decision. People always have suggestions and sympathy in abundance for the seekers. If you fail, you would be satisfied that you listened to your inner voice and had the guts to take that step.

You are born the day you find the purpose of your life. Before that, you just exist.

Push yourself. Don't be dependent on anyone. People can make you smile, not happy from within. It's only you who has the ability to feel the happiness inside.

The only person standing between your dreams and your success is you.

If you choose to be good, the next time, be better. Keep enhancing your expectation levels from yourself, against yourself.

To be better than the best, make perfection your addiction.

Don't be dependent on anyone, be it for happiness or for the realization of your dreams. It's your job and only you have to pursue it. So...

Own your way, your own way.

4

Karma haunts.
Be good, do good.

❧

May your Profit & Loss account
of deeds for humanity
be in profits;
for you have to present
your balance sheet
on the Judgment Day.

❖

Always be fair and good to yourself and others. Do good and help* people as much as you can. Be genuine while making decisions, without pre-judging anyone.

*Conditions apply. Don't allow others to take undue advantage of your helping nature.

Kindness is the basic ingredient for the recipe of happiness.

Your one act of kindness can make someone's day. And real happiness is in making someone smile.

Good things happen to good people; have faith.

Karma is not only in doing good, it's also about spreading the good. If someone does something wrong to you, try to forgive them.

Happiness is…forgiving the mistake of others and apologizing for yours.

❖

This story would make you believe that karma does exist.

A guy named Nick had shifted from his hometown to a metropolitan city for his first job. He was in search of an accommodation for which his friends and acquaintances helped him, but nothing materialized. A property agent referred by one of his friends finally helped him in searching for a flat. He showed Nick five or six flats as per his budget and that too near the office location.

As the deal was finalised, the agent requested him, "Sir! Can you please refer more people who need accommodation?"

"Ok," replied Nick, casually looking at a flat in the next street from his balcony that was still under construction. "This one would be amazing when complete. I liked the layout."

"That one?" the agent peeped out and pointed it out with his index finger. "The owner knows me. If you want that, I can arrange it for you. But after six months only."

"Oh," Nick raised his brows. "But I can't wait for six months."

"Yes!" the agent laughed giving him the keys, "Refer me clients please, I'll give them some discount and also give you commission for every reference."

"Commission?" laughed Nick thumping his shoulder. "That's great, and thanks for offering, but it's okay my friend. I will refer people if they are searching for an accommodation. No need to pay me anything for it."

Two years passed.

During that time, Nick had referred many colleagues and friends to the agent. But now, Nick too was searching for a bigger accommodation as his brother was also shifting to the city with him. He called up the agent.

"Hey brother! How are you?" he said.

"Good my friend," replied the agent. "You got another reference?"

"Yup, this time it's me," he said and smiled.

"Why?" The agent was surprised. "Did the landlord say something? Is there an issue I can help with?"

"No, no. Nothing like that. I just need a bigger flat as my brother is also shifting with me now."

"I have one flat near the roundabout and one behind the market. Which one do you want?"

"These two you had shown earlier as well and I had not liked them much," Nick said politely.

"Don't worry, I'll search a good one for you," the agent promised.

"By the way, how much has your commission increased by?"

"My friend," laughed the agent, "You've referred so many clients to me till now that I will not mind even if you don't pay."

"It's nice of you, but let's keep friendship and business separate. You should let me know your charges."

"Okay, if you insist, you can pay me fifty percent of the commission that I charge from others, fine?"

"Sounds good."

"I will call you in two days."

In the meanwhile, Nick continued his own search for the flat and asked his friends and colleagues too for the same. He shortlisted two places on his own but waited for the agent's call to see the options.

After waiting for another day, he called up the agent, "Hi! Any luck?"

"Not much."

"I saw one, but rent is higher than I had assumed," Nick said.

"Which one are you talking about?"

"There's one in street number ten; newly constructed."

"Oh! The one I had shown you?" the agent confirmed.

"Haha yeah! When there were just heaps of sand and bricks all around it."

"Yes yes! That one only," the agent said and laughed. "I didn't refer that to you because your budget is not that much."

"Hmm." Nick sighed. "But there is no other good option nearby. I am thinking if I rent a place a bit far, then I would spend money on travelling. The time I would waste is of more value than the rent itself. So maybe I should loosen my pocket a bit and increase my budget. What do you say?"

"Okay then," the agent said, "I'll talk to the owner and ask the rent and other things."

"I have already talked to him."

"Oh! What did he say?"

"He said I can shift in a week's time."

"Nice!" the agent prompted. "But I'll talk to the owner again."

"I have already talked to him, so I think I will just pay the token money today."

"No brother," the agent said, "Why will you pay the token money? I'll handle it."

"Ok. So let's finalise it this weekend only."

"Sure!"

"Could you please arrange an agreement for the same? I'll pay the charges."

"Don't worry brother, that's included in the commission."

"Commission?"

"Yes," the agent laughed. "You forgot I have given you only a fifty percent discount. The rest you'll need to pay."

"One sec," Nick asked him, "Which commission?"

"My commission for arranging the flat on rent."

"Dude!" Nick chuckled, "I have talked to the owner directly, not through you."

"Brother, I had shown the flat to you. The rent is so high, so I can't let go of half the commission."

Nick couldn't help laughing, "My friend, you had shown me the flat two years back, when it was under construction. Not even a tent had been placed there to stay in."

"But I am the agent for this area and the owner would let out through me only."

"Sorry?" Nick was confused, "I contacted the owner as he has placed a To-Let board on his property. Ok!"

"See!" the agent replied in a serious tone, "If you want to shift, you'll have to pay me the commission."

"Oh, is it?" Nick was astonished. "Seriously man? This is…I mean…seriously?"

"Yes!" the agent replied in anger now. "Seriously yes."

Nick started laughing again.

"Did I crack a joke? You have to…"

The agent was about to complete his words, but Nick disconnected the call.

Later, Nick dialled up his mother back home for a chit chat and shared the conversation he had had with the agent.

His mother advised him, "Don't mess with property dealers. Take some other flat."

"Oh mom! Come on!" He laughed it away. "He was talking nonsense. Anyway, he is not a gangster and more so, I am not the hero of a movie who knows boxing and would just start a fight. It'll be okay."

After disconnecting the call, Nick got busy with arranging his daily stuff. Then he dialled the grocery store, "Can you please deliver one brown bread, a dozen eggs, golden ones, and and and... milk," he said and gave his address.

After half an hour, the doorbell rang. Nick placed the laptop aside and got up. The bell was rung again.

"Coming!" Nick yelled.

Immediately thereafter, the bell rang again. "He thinks he is a CEO or what, getting late for the AGM? Silly guy." Nick murmured rushing towards the door.

He opened the door saying, "Can't you wai...?"

Nick was shocked to see that the person standing in front of him was not the grocery delivery chap, but the property agent. His eyes were red, though not with anger. He seemed drunk.

"Why did you disconnect my call?" asked the agent in a husky voice.

"Simple!" Nick raised his shoulders, "I just didn't want to talk to you."

"Why?" the agent said, raising his hand up.

Nick had a lump in his throat as he saw his hand. He was holding a knife. His physical strength was not enough for this fat drunk man equipped with a mutton chopper.

"See!" Nick fumbled gathering courage to speak, "I...I... actually. I am sorry. But..."

"But?" the agent yelled.

A chill ran through Nick's spine, but he managed to speak, "If you want me not to shift...then..."

"Then?" the agent yelled again.

"Then..." Nick moved a step back, "Then...I will not shift in that flat."

"But why did you disconnect the call?" the agent screamed at his loudest, scaring him. The agent then stepped ahead and punched Nick in the jaw.

"Ah!" Nick sat down holding the chair, groaning in pain. Blood spurted from his gums.

The agent bent down, held Nick from the collar, pulled him up and put the knife at his chin. Nick looked straight into his eyes. It seemed as if he was staring at his death. He could see the agent's revengeful eyes, which he could never have imagined.

"I always treated you as a good friend," said Nick.

The agent was still red-eyed, seemed to be burning with anger.

"I helped you out a lot in the last two years," Nick continued while his lips bled, "I gave you so many referrals and you earned so much with my help."

The agent stood frozen.

"Is this what I deserve?" Nick asked coughing, struggling to breathe as his collar was noosed. "Is this how you treat a friend who never asked for anything in return?"

The agent stood motionless.

Nick added, "You call me a friend and I address you as brother."

The agent dropped the knife and released Nick's collar, stepping back. Nick coughed again holding his neck as he could finally breathe.

Within a moment, the agent came back to Nick, picked up the knife, clamped his hands around Nick's jaw and shouted, "We are not friends anymore."

"Ah!" Nick grunted in pain, "Okay...okay!"

"Huh!" The agent pushed Nick away and went out of the house, banging the door behind him.

Nick took a sigh of relief but was still in shock at what had happened to him and wondered why it had happened. When he came back to his senses, he pulled a cloth and covered his jaw and moved quickly towards his study table for his mobile phone.

He had picked up the phone to call the police, but he heard a loud noise outside, followed by much commotion. He rushed towards the kitchen window to see what had happened. It was a biker, who had rammed into someone and people has gathered around.

"He is drunk," said the biker pointing at the person on the footpath, holding his leg, groaning in pain. "It was his mistake," said the biker to the people gathered there. "He rushed onto the road from this building and came in front of me."

The man lying on the road was groaning in pain with something stuck on his thigh. Nick moved ahead to check and noticed that it was the agent. The thing stuck in his thigh was nothing else but the same knife he had been holding.

❖

A fortnight later, Nick was moving his luggage into the new flat. The agent was in one corner of the street, sitting on a wheel chair, with a cast on his leg. He was guiding a few people who were helping Nick move his belongings into the new flat. After all the stuff had been moved from the old flat to the new, Nick came to the agent.

"Thank you brother!" said Nick looking in his eyes and smiled, "Thank you so much for asking your friends to help me move my stuff."

The agent smiled holding his hand, "My friend! *Good things happen to good people*," and he indicated towards his plastered leg, "And sometimes bad things also happen to good people," and they laughed.

"Also, thank you for asking my old landlord to give me an extra week to stay," added Nick.

"I don't understand…," the agent said confused.

"I mean, the new landlord took another week to let out his flat and the old landlord wanted me to shift so…"

As he was about to complete, the agent said, "No no! Not that, I am asking something else."

"Oh, sorry. What?"

"You know, doctors told me had I got delayed in getting hospitalised that day, I would have lost my leg."

Nick smiled and patted the agent's shoulder. "Don't worry, everything is fine now."

"I am sorry," the agent pleaded. "I did bad to you that day. I was drunk and had lost my mind over a brawl. I am really sorry."

"It's ok!" Nick thumped his shoulder. "Leave it, that's gone now."

"But I don't understand…why did you take me to the doctor?"

Nick smiled and said, *"What people do to you is their Karma; what you do to them is yours."*

❖

The above story and many alike prove the following quote:

Karma haunts.

You'll get back, directly or indirectly, what you do to others.

Reacting to someone's harsh words is like playing with the chewing-gum thrown by someone.

Had the guy reacted to the agent's words and fought back, he may have only won the fight. Instead, he won over the agent with his words and got what he wanted. Moreover, he also got an extended stay in the previous landlord's place, though with the help of the same agent who had treated him badly.

Karma is not only about doing good, but also not reacting to the bad done by people.

Forgive people because you believe in a life larger than revenge.

Praising others whole heartedly makes you happy from within. The agent realised his *Karma* and helped Nick in the best possible way.

When you make someone happy, especially the unhappy ones, that moment you define humanity.

Life is larger than just taking revenge and brooding over the bad that happened to you in the past.

Happiness is…capturing the pictures called moments, from the lens called experiences, with the camera called vision, on the canvas called life.

5

Life is like a guitar: Tune. Play. Repeat.

⚜

Life is like a guitar
and the combination of chords
are called moments.
Playing them is called
living the moments.

❖

Once there was a boy who was fascinated by music, especially the guitar. He was so mesmerised by the strumming of strings that one day he asked his father to buy him a guitar. His father happily obliged. Ben was so excited to play it that he picked it up and started strumming right away. He was very happy, enjoying the moment.

He learnt a few essential tips about playing a guitar from online videos and started off. He would play a new song everyday for his parents at night before sleep. Though he was not that good as a beginner, his parents always appreciated his efforts. His friends, especially the girls in his gang, were impressed with his newly-adopted hobby. He felt like a rock star while playing birthday jingles and on-demand songs at events and night-outs.

A few months later, his passion seemed to be mellowing down. He would hardly pick up the guitar; he would rather be busy with his gaming console or chatting. Not seeing him passionate about his guitar rehearsals as he had been in the past, his father asked one day, "What's wrong? I don't see you playing your guitar anymore. It's either lying by your side or you are holding it but busy chatting on your phone, like now."

"I don't know," he shrugged. "I don't like playing it anymore."

"Why?" his father was surprised at the sudden confession.

"I think I'm not good at it," he replied sadly, pushing the guitar aside.

"But you told me you want it badly, and I guess it was going fine."

"Yeah!" He nodded with the head down. "It was, but I don't know how to play like a pro. There is a guy in our school, and he plays so amazingly. His fingers move so quickly on the fret board, everyone is impressed with him. Even my bestie is impressed with him and she says I stand nowhere in front of him."

"Oh! That's the matter," his father came and sat by him.

"I try and rehearse a lot, but I am not able to pick up pace," Ben complained.

"Why don't you join weekend guitar classes? That will help you."

"But," he said showing him the mobile, "I am good at playing. I learnt it all from these downloaded apps."

"Learn it from someone who plays it amazingly, like you said. This app can't tell where you are going wrong."

Ben pondered over his father's words at night. The very next day, he found a guitar teacher and started taking lessons.

He took lessons for a month and his interest and passion rekindled, with perfection this time. He practiced every day and got better than before.

"Happy now?" asked his father seeing him playing with his friends at home.

"Yup dad! See what they gifted me," Ben said, showing the heart-shaped plectrum with his photo on it.

His father saw that and said, "I think your bestie gave it?" He nodded smiling.

Ben had been attending all sessions with the professional guitar tutor sincerely. He had also been practicing regularly, and playing it in front of his friends and family members.

But, his passion for playing the guitar could survive for a few weeks, after which he was back to square one. He picked up the guitar very rarely.

"Now what?" asked his father, "Why did you stop playing the guitar now?"

"I don't enjoy it anymore."

"And the reason?" his father asked thoughtfully.

"I can't make it sound right," he replied twitching his cheeks. "I forget chords while playing. I practice, I work hard and I'm patient. But still, in the end, I get nothing but this," he said showing cuts on his fingers.

His dad smiled, picked up the guitar and sat beside him. He strummed a chord with an index finger and asked, "When did you tune it last?"

"I don't know," he sighed.

"Do you know how to play the seven basic notes of any chord?" His father plucked out a new chord with his ring finger.

"I do, but…"

"But what?"

"I'll have to revise."

"Maybe," said dad, putting the guitar back. "You should take a step back from it for a while."

"No!" the boy said surprised. "I want to learn it, dad. If I take a break, I won't be able to pick it up again."

"Son," his father said running his hand through Ben's hair, "There are three rules of playing."

Tune. Play. Repeat.

"One – You never tune it before you play, so its sound annoys you. Part of your warm up is tuning.

"Two – You don't learn the ABCs of the guitar, and just want to cram the chords. That's why you forget the finger placement while playing. You must first learn the fundamentals.

"Three – You don't take a break and freshen up your mind. Even your mind needs rest some times."

❖

The above story is especially for guitar lovers.

But imagine if the same rules of guitar are applied to life, then what would be the outcome? Won't life be more meaningful and interesting?

Live life full time.

They say, "You only live once." This might be true, but there is another perspective to life called "*Living beyond life*" which defines that a person lives many times, every moment, even after life. The person lives in the words of others, in books, in examples that others quote. But all this is possible only when life is lived to its fullest. And that is possible only when people are passionate about the things they do.

Behind every successful flight, lies the will, full of thrust, against the wind; the will to win.

The will to win comes only when people enjoy the things they do and to enjoy the things, rules of guitar can be an apt example.

Tune. Play. Repeat.

Here are the three rules of Guitar vis-à-vis Life, in detail:

a) **Tune:** You might have seen a guitarist fiddling with the strings of his guitar, loosening or tightening the screws fixed on the head of the guitar. That is called tuning.

Before playing the guitar, a guitarist first tunes it, so that it produces the sounds at preset frequency to be in sync with rules of music called notes, i.e. Sa Re Ga Ma Pa Dha Ni Sa or C D E F G A B C, etc.

Similarly, in life too, first you need to *tune* yourself. You need to prepare yourself before you start anything or something new. The same rule also applies when you re-start something old with a new style or method, or say a grand invention.

You win, not by defeating others, but by performing better than before.

To perform the best, or better than before, you need to be prepared. And for that, you need to know the fundamental building blocks. If you want to start a business, then know the market, research your competitors, how and why your product is different from others. If you are a job seeker, update yourself with various and newest interview tips, tricks and latest topics related to your field; make your CV stand out from the others so that it makes an impression. If you are a student, chalk out a time table for your studies. What matters is not just a study plan, but selecting a place of study plays a vital role too. Create a space that attracts you when you study. Arranging a study table near the window that gives you a glimpse to the open sky – especially a quiet place, like towards the garden – can be the best place to start with.

If you are about to start working on your dreams, make sure you have enough reserves to pay your bills, for you may have to invest before you start earning from your dream project. If you don't know what your dreams are, as happens with many, then you need to check what it is that would give you immense pleasure.

The best way to check what you want is to first imagine that you have nothing and then check if the thing you want really matters to you. Your priorities would change; your wishes would change for sure.

Make a list of all the things you love doing, all your hobbies. Strike off the ones you are not passionate about. Zero in upon the one that you are best at, the one that doesn't make you feel bored at all. And then research more about that passion. Know how to start it, jot down all the pros and cons. Once finalised, prepare yourself, and tune yourself to start it. The sooner, the better.

Whatever you do, do it with passion; learn new things, set new standards. If you fall down, get up; just get going, non-stop. This is how dreams come true.

To tune your life and the goals, you should know the very basics. If you learn how things work and also the way they don't, you'll be better equipped for success.

So once you know the *what* and *how* of your passion, jump off the bridge. The question *why* needs no answer; it's a no brainer, it's simple – You *love* it, and that's enough reason to pursue it.

If the string of the guitar breaks, you should have a backup ready. Likewise, have a business continuity plan (BCP) ready for your venture. Or should we call it the DCP, the Dream's Continuity Plan. More than BCP or DCP, the biggest thing to stay away from is negativity. It's good to be prepared and to have a back-up plan, but don't over-think things.

Negativity pierces determination like rust. Stay coated with faith and confidence.

Once you are tuned, the next door would open up by itself.

b) **Play:** Once you are done with tuning the guitar of your dream life, and you know the ABC of playing it, just *play* it. Give it your best shot.

Taking the first step to roll the wheel of your dreams needs just one thing: Play your heart out.

The only person standing between your dreams and making them a reality is you.

So *you* and only *you* need to play it. Don't expect others to do it for you. Nobody else can achieve your dream for you. If you wait for that, you'll be screwed. The other person would either enjoy it, or have just one thing for your failure – sympathy.

Make mistakes flawlessly, and improve progressively.

Get a mentor, but make it a DIY project, that is Do It Yourself. Learn from others, discuss your progress with friends, family or likeminded people, take suggestions...but remember, it has to be a DIY thing.

If you have tried it before, learn from your mistakes and play it better this time. Keep in mind your ultimate goal and walk that road. Stay focussed, without thinking too much about obstacles and worrying about the past and future; be in the present.

Live in the NOW. *Live life to its fullest. Don't spend more than 10% of your time learning from the past, and 20% planning for the future. Live in the present, act* NOW *to fulfil the dreams you plan.*

The tunes you play should have the impact to bring change. So learn the right song and bring about that change with your original and lively ideas.

Change is growth, movement is change; keep moving, keep growing.

c) **Repeat:** Once you have achieved your goal or a level of satisfaction is there, take some time to rest. Recline you chair and see the path you have travelled before you *repeat* the rule (a) above.

The moment you stop and look around, you will get to know that you have so many small moments full of happiness. So just be thankful, as many others don't have these moments. There are also some who do, but can't visualize them; and even some who have, but can't appreciate them.

Gift yourself a break to sit back and relax. Cherish the moments that you felt while playing the tunes straight from your heart.

Dream and sleep.

See bigger dreams while you relax. Don't settle; your dreams won't become a reality on their own just because you achieved a level or crossed a milestone. Dream big, move and bring about change to reach your dream.

The best gift to give yourself is to just be yourself, and improving on the person that you were yesterday.

Before repeating, take an account of all the mistakes and learn from them. Make sure you repeat the rule (a) above and not the mistakes. If the mistakes result into problems, remember:

When problems come, stay calm under these two situations. One, when you know you can solve them, so smile; two, when you know you can't do anything to change it, so be calm.

Once you have taken some time off, done with your analysis of how you have performed, rewarded yourself a cookie or two for your hard work, get back to business: *repeat.*

6

Tame the time...
before it tames you.

༄

Let yourself be
the disciple of time
and see how
the beautiful world
of your dreams
emerges around you.

❖

Just visualising a goal is not enough; spending value time on it is the key element. It's not always necessary for you to be earning from your hobby, but don't seek *synthetic happiness*: time spent for temporary amusements like movies or outings or weekends on a beach is all synthetic. Such happiness has a shelf life of a day or two. Work for your bigger dreams that encapsulate an entire lifetime. Then movies and beach holidays would seem more interesting.

❖

Here is a beautiful story.

Once there was a child named Roy. He asked his father for a daily allowance. His father looked at him and replied, "I am not concerned with giving you money, but my concern is what you would spend it on."

Roy replied innocently, "Whenever you'll be back from office at night, I would show you what I bought with it. Promise."

The father smiled and said, "Okay! But there are two conditions: One, I shall take back the money that is unspent. Two, you can sell me the things at double the price you bought, if I like them. Also, I'll deduct your pocket money for double the price of the things you waste money on."

Roy thought about it, grimaced, but agreed to it saying, "I need ten dollars minimum."

His father thought for a while curling his lips and replied, "I'll give you fourteen dollars and forty cents."

The boy's jaw dropped at the offer and he readily agreed, hugging his father out of sheer joy.

The next day when Roy woke up, he found $14.40 under his pillow. In the evening when the father came back, the kid showed him his bag. It contained toffees, toys, and chocolates. His father didn't like or dislike anything, but still asked, "Have you spent all of the money?"

Roy smiled showing his pockets inside out.

The same thing happened for the entire week. Roy spent all of the pocket money. The father didn't buy or dislike anything. On the first day of the second week, Roy bought some good stuff. At night, when his father came home, his son showed him some of the gifts. When the father opened the bag, he loved what was inside: a paper weight. As pre-decided, the father gave him double of the value for paper-weight.

The second day, when his father came from the office, his son gave him a few gifts again and some money he couldn't spend.

"Why didn't you spend all?" asked the father.

"I was not prepared with my new list. I didn't want to buy the same old stuff," replied Neil sadly.

On the third day, when the father came back home, Roy showed him some more toys and candies.

"I didn't like your spending the amount on the same stuff, more so when you don't like the stuff…you had said that a couple of days back yourself. So I'll deduct double the money of some stuff," replied his father. The same happened for the next two-three days. Now Roy owed some money to his father.

That night, his father told him, "I'll waive off your debt if you spend the pocket money tomorrow wisely."

Next night, Roy stood waiting for his father, empty handed.

"What did you buy today?" he asked.

"I gave it to my friend for cycle repair," Roy replied softly.

"And what did he give you in return?"

"Nothing."

"Why?" his father asked in anger.

"Because I like her."

"Oh!" his father was surprised. "It's a she."

Roy nodded innocently.

His father held his chin with love and asked, "What would you do if I give you money tomorrow?"

"I don't know how to use it." Roy hugged his father. "You spend it for me."

❖

Now, imagine you are that kid and the daily pocket money of $14.40 is actually the 1,440 minutes, i.e. 24 hours of a day.

This story has five takeaways.

First: Whatever time you don't use, won't stay with you. It goes wasted, like Roy's unspent money, because he had to return it to his father.

Second: If you give your valuable time to others and others like it, they would give you their valuable time and love. Like when Roy bought the paper weight for his father, and the father gave him a hug and double the money of the paperweight's cost.

Third: If you give your valuable time to the person in genuine need, even if you don't get anything material in return, that shall give you happiness, like the son helped his friend to get her cycle repaired.

Fourth: If you waste time, you would have to further spend your tomorrow in repairing the loss occurred due to wasted time. Like Roy was indebted to his father for double the price of items he didn't like, which was deducted from his next day's pocket money.

Fifth: If you don't know how to manage or put your time to value, get advice from experienced ones. Just like the son surrendered the idea of managing his allowance to his father.

So use time well, spend it wisely on yourself, your family, friends, and others.

Making someone smile would make your day.

Keep track of time. You do not have to become a calendar or a wall clock, chanting the seconds of the day. Learning how to keep track of time spent on your dream is enough.

Mark the progress of your goal in your calendar. Progress in terms of revenue or growth in employees, or pages written if you are an author, etc., can be measured easily rather than setting a vague non-measurable and impossible to achieve target.

Set a deadline for your project or milestone so that you can compare your *status quo* scenario of dreams from the start date.

From the day you had nothing to when you get something big or say everything, is the period you live your life at the best. Keep evolving.

First nurture your leisure time in the things you love doing or you always wanted to do but never had the time for. Your life will become more fulfilling once you taste the satisfaction that your passion gives you. That passion will become addicting with the passage of time.

Passion rejuvenates.

Whether you're painting, playing guitar, writing, blogging or even bird watching, once you get the feel of your passion in your routine, you won't be so focused on completing a milestone. You would be addicted to it. You shall cherish every moment you spend working for your passion.

May you live long, but suppose it's your last day in this world. Any regrets you would have for the things you didn't do? List them, for these are your dreams. Start living them...NOW!

Time slips by. Just five minutes spent towards achieving your goal every day would gradually increase to two hours of dedication within one month. You would never regret having given those five minutes to your dream then.

7

Friendship is divine...
think anything, get everything.

❧

Friends understand the unsaid words,
no matter if they are silent for years.

❖

You need family and friends to go back and relax with. Nothing else can give you a sense of comfort and belonging. It is essential to take some time out of your busy life to connect with friends frequently. The moment you fail or win, you need someone to talk to and share your emotions of that moment with. Who better than those who love you without expectations.

Family members are the first friends and friends are like second family.

While making friends, you need not be very choosy. Nor do you need to create a list as to what to see while befriending someone. All you need to do is stop being with those who de-motivate you, people who kill your happiness. Stop running after the wrong people who don't deserve your attention or care.

The right person, who feels like being there with you, will be with you. Stop insisting the wrong ones. Period.

❖

Here is a heart touching story of two friends: Joy, a rich guy and Tony, a poor guy.

One of them was more studious, Tony; he had no money to spend on video games or movies and outings, so the best pastime became studying.

At the cusp of passing out of school, both started thinking about which courses to study that would best fit their areas of interest. As per their interests, they zeroed in on the stream to pursue, and eventually made a list of the reputed colleges to go to.

Joy suggested taking admission in a famous college known for its campus placements. Tony hesitated because it was more than he could afford. He chose not to fill out an application for that college saying, "I will go to a government college, the one my cousin suggested."

Joy prompted, "You are good at studies. You'll get shortlisted by the college. The problem, if any, will arise for me, for I won't fit their minimum cut-off criteria." But Tony was confident of his decision.

"Okay," said Joy, "I will join with you, wherever you go."

"Why?" Tony was surprised, "You can join any private college you want."

"Are you coming with me or not?" Joy asked.

Tony had no choice but to follow him. They filled out an application for two colleges, one private and one government.

On the day that a list of selected candidates was to be put up, they visited the private college. Joy scrolled through the names listed on the notice board. He yelled as he found Tony's name, "Buddy! You are selected."

The very next moment he yelled, "God! My name is not there."

He came back to Tony who was waiting near the admission fee counter. When he saw Tony sad, he consoled him, "You are sad because my name is not there in the list. I am proud of you. You are my true and best friend."

"I am not sad because of that...," Tony said surprised.

"What?" Joy was slightly taken aback.

Tony smirked, "I am sad because only my name is there."

"Rascal!" Joy kicked him playfully. "Don't you worry, I'll get admission somehow. We'll rock in this college."

Since there was a long queue at the admission counter, they went for a lunch break. But when they came back, the admission fee counter was closed and the cashier asked them to visit the next day.

Due to some medical emergency in Tony's family, he missed visiting the next day, after which the admissions were closed to the private college. It left Tony with no other option but to go for another college that was not much recognised.

Joy called him later and told Tony that he had secured admission in that private college. Happy for his friend, Tony congratulated him, "Great! But please concentrate on studies only. Not the girls around."

"I'll try," Joy smirked. "Anyway, when are you going for admissions?"

"Another college would open the admissions tomorrow."

"Do you want me to come along?" asked Joy.

"Nope, I'll manage."

The next day Tony was standing in the queue, a really long one. He felt thirsty so asked the guy standing next to him to reserve his place. He turned around to go, but the guy standing behind him in crowd offered him his water bottle.

"It's ok! Thank you, I'll..." Tony replied, taking a step out of the queue, but then stopped as he recognised the voice. He looked behind with joy. It was Joy.

"What are you doing here?" asked Tony.

"Could you please fill this for me?" smiled Joy, giving Tony an unfilled admission form that carried his photo.

"Are you mad?" he pulled the form from him.

"Sort of, but not like you," he quipped. "How dare you think that I would study without you?"

"And your admission in that college?"

Joy laughed, "I love pranks."

"But why? You could have managed admission there very easily," Tony almost shouted.

"Because I don't want you to top every time in every semester. I'll give you tough competition this year."

"You are an idiot." Tony was angry, yet overwhelmed.

"Done?" said Joy pulling a pen from Tony's pocket giving it to him, "Now fill it up and get back to the queue. Next is our turn."

"Excuse me!" said a pretty girl approaching Joy. "Do you have a pen please?"

"Yes!" said Joy, pulling the pen out of Tony's hand. He then asked her politely, "Could I have the pleasure to fill this form for you?"

Tony stood looking at him, bewildered, and Joy made faces moving with the girl to fill up her form.

Ten years later

Tony got out of a big car. He was holding an admission form. He came to his child's school's guest area. His child was walking behind him, holding the hand of a beautiful lady, the child's mother.

A teacher came to them and asked, "Could you please fill out the form?"

The lady next to Tony took the pen from Tony's pocket.

The kid asked her, "Mom, can I try?" and started filling out the form.

Another kid came and snatched his pen, placing a form on the desk, "First fill mine, then yours."

Tony looked at him and then the couple who followed him. Tony smiled as he saw them. They were Joy and his wife.

A few moments later, a little girl came to the kids and asked, "Do you have a pen please?"

Junior Joy looked at junior Tony and indicated him to give the pen.

Junior Tony shook his head and hid the pen behind his back.

Joy's wife prompted, "Give it to her honey, this is how friends sacrifice."

Joy giggled and said, "Yeah, I am still bearing the punishment of the sacrifice that day when I pulled the pen from my best friend's hand and filled the admission form of my would-be-best-friend." He looked into his wife's eyes and she elbowed him with a smile.

Tony went to Joy and whispered, "Thank me that I didn't tell her all your secrets, else she wouldn't have agreed to be even friends with you."

Joy raised his brows, "You know nothing about my secrets and I know nothing about yours."

"Oh hello!" Tony raised his brows, "I don't have any, ok!"

"Whatever! Your future secrets."

"She would know all," prompted Tony and Joy continued teasing whim with his baseless arguments.

Mrs. Joy giggled, "I am jealous sometimes; they seem to be like soul-mates."

"Me too," replied Mrs. Tony with a smile.

"But happy to have great friends like Tony and you," Mrs. Joy added holding the other's hand.

❖

Friends are like flowers. They carry the fragrance called happiness.

Make two best friends at every stage of your life, and that's it. Three is a gang and four is a crowd.

The rule of friendship is: no rules in friendship.

Choose friends carefully and wisely. Find the ones who connect with your heart, who actually understand you, even if you don't put your thoughts in words. Don't concentrate on making new friends only; call up the old ones you haven't seen in a few years. Connect with them, hang around if you get a chance, even if it is only once a year or two.

Friends are like camcorders of your life. They see the track you follow and the destination you are heading towards. Consult them, share with them, ask them, blame them, irritate them, smile with them, cry with them, talk nonsense, and laugh.

Friendship is divine: think anything, get everything.

8

*Be with parents, always;
for they spend their whole life
for your better life.*

❧

*Sometimes, a father becomes
the most emotional mom on earth;
and mother, the strongest dad.*

❖

Parents do not demand anything but your presence. In case you are living away and meeting them is not possible on daily basis, then visit them at decent intervals. So we should be with them for as much time as we can.

Parents were always there when you were growing up, so be with them while they grow old.

Visit them often, attend even the smallest of occasions that are special to them, just for their happiness. Make all the events memorable for them. If there is any good news coming up, take them by surprise.

The longest tenured first LOVE and greatest TEACHER, in fact life long, is none the other than the Mother.

Dad will be dad. Sometimes he is strict, but he loves silently, for his care is wrapped up in all the hard work he does to give his children a great bringing up.

❖

Here is a real story (name changed) that would make you realise the reality of life which is ignored in the race of growth. It would change the dimension of your busy life.

This is the story of John, the CEO of one of the biggest automobile companies who left his home country and moved to one of the richest Middle-East countries. We both connected over official matters, but that official connection grew to a friendly connect because we both had similar thoughts about life and spirituality.

I got a chance to visit the country he was settled in for business reasons. After my meetings, as I got free in the evening I dialled his number.

"Hello! Could I talk to Mr. John please?"

"Hi! Speaking. Who is this?"

"Someone has sent this book titled *10 Alone* for you all the way from India."

"*Habibi Habibi Habibi* (friend)!" He laughed and said, "How are you?"

"Oh, amazing sir! You recognised me?"

"Only you can play a prank on me like this, my friend," he laughed again. "So, you are back? How are you?"

"Smart, as usual sir." I smirked. "Thank you! How are you?"

"Good one. I like it. So! What brings you here?"

"Some connections, some friends."

"Ha ha ha! Good to hear. Let's meet when you are free."

"Always free for you sir," I said checking my bag if I had my novel with me.

"Good! Text me your hotel address. We'll go to the city for dinner."

"Cool! Or maybe I'll reach directly. Gonna meet my friends, they'll drop me there."

"That'll be just fine."

On my way back to the hotel, I texted him my hotel location. After freshening up, I had a quick catch-up with a few of my old friends and colleagues and then was free by eight.

I reached the venue he had sent in the text and texted him, "I have reached."

"I am in the parking," the text blinked on my mobile.

"*Habibi!*" he said coming with open arms. "How are you?"

"All well sir. *Shukran*, you tell," I said hugging him.

"Oh! You still remember Arabic a bit?"

"Few years, few friends and a few words," I said and we laughed.

"Let's go to the rooftop area."

We settled there amidst the dim-lit tables with people enjoying their hookahs and Arabic food.

"What would you like to have?" he asked passing the menu over to me.

"Thank you sir," I turned it back to him saying, "I am bad at ordering, so please help me get the best one."

"Ha ha," he picked up the menu, "Let me order the speciality of this place, one of the Arabic dishes I am sure you'll like."

While he placed the order, I noticed he had maintained the same humbleness. He still seemed to be an all contended person.

"So how is your family?" I asked as he was done with placing the order.

"Oh they are good," he replied putting his car keys, mobile, a branded huge-dial gold plated watch and wallet aside. "My daughter completed internship after graduation in New York; my son is going to complete his pilot training in the US."

"Wow, that's amazing. All happily pursuing their passions."

"Umm yup," he smiled back. I was about to ask about his wife but I noticed him thinking, which made me go quiet.

The sumptuously delightful dinner was served by the team of waiters who not only decorated the plates with food but also placed a message of the day innovatively written on the salad. It read -

"*You are known by the thoughts you seed...* and the salad you eat."

"Awesome," I said with excitement at the out-of-the-box thinking of the restaurant staff.

"Yeah! Just taste the food and you'll be short of words."

"Out of the world," I said astonished as I had the first bite. "I haven't had such tasty food ever... but..."

"But?" he curved his brows.

"But this is still at number two in my list of the best. The *karela* (bitter gourd) fried by my mom is number one."

"Yeah! Even my mom used to turn all tasteless vegetables into lip smacking dishes."

I could see that he was missing his mother. Just to cheer up the mood, I giggled and said,

"*These days, a girl would marry a guy who cooks amazing karela, and a guy would marry a girl who won't ask him to eat karelas.*"

"Ha ha!" he was back to normal with that silly joke. "You know, my family always prefers this restaurant whenever they visit me."

"Oh cool. So how frequently do they visit you?"

"My wife visits me often," he said asking for rice. I passed it over to him and he continued, "She visits once in every two months, for three or four days."

"That's nice," I managed to smile, "And kids?"

"Their mom and I visited our son two months back and before that we went to New York to see our daughter."

"Cool, all settled, visiting places, great life you have made for yourself and your family."

He began laughing lightly, and immediately started coughing.

"Easy easy!" I got up and thumped his back and gave him water. The waiter too rushed to us, "Sir! Are you fine?"

"Ugh Ugh! Yes I am fine, thank you," he said pulling the tissue papers and directing me back to my chair. "You please have a seat, I am all right."

"I am so sorry," I said coming back to my seat. "I am a chatter box. I forget the basics... not to talk while eating. So Sorry."

"That's fine! You need not be," he said picking the bowl, "May be I am used to having food in silence."

I looked at him and noticed the disturbed silence of his eyes behind the gold plated spectacles.

We finished dinner and went to the buffet section to pick our choice of desserts.

"This is *Harissa*, the Arabic semolina cake," he said putting that in his plate.

"I think you should not have sweets," I said looking at his plate, "Two pieces?"

"Hey!" He was surprised. "How did you know I am not allowed sweets?"

"Sugar free was slipping out from your wallet on the table."

"Ha ha ha! Shh! Don't tell anyone," he said and winked.

"Don't worry, your wife is not here," I smiled at what I thought was a good joke.

I noticed his eyes. It seemed as if he said silently, "I wish she was here."

We went back to the table and had the sweets. He seemed to be quiet.

"So when are you visiting India?" I asked to break the silence.

He was busy having the sweets or may be pretending to be busy or lost in some other thoughts.

"Mr. John!"

"Hmm? Yes! You said something?" He shook his head coming out of his thoughts.

"I asked when are you visiting India?"

"Soon," he smiled, or tried to.

I could guess the emptiness in his feelings.

After the dinner, we went out. He clicked the button on his car key and the blinkers tweeted.

"Oh! You drive this one?" I said looking at the king size head turner car.

"Yes!"

"Great!" I was amazed. "I am not that crazy about SUVs but this one is breathtaking. Big boy's toy."

"I used to be crazy, once upon a time."

"Oh! This is the result of that once upon a time?"

"Right! Once upon a time," he said and sighed.

"But you made your dream come true."

"Oh yes, I realised my dreams, but I realised quite late that these dreams were temporary, just like a person's first crush. Infatuation, you know?"

Our conversation had taken a serious turn. Rather than getting in the car, we stood there.

"John, can I ask you something if you don't mind?" I asked leaning on the car.

"Sure, tell me," he said putting all his stuff like the mobile, car keys and wallet on the bonnet.

"How do you feel today if you look back and see the success you have won for yourself?"

He smiled touching the dial of his golden watch and said, "My wrist has seen so many watches, from rubber straps to golden ones; just one thing is constant."

"And what is that?"

"Time," he looked straight in my eyes, with a smile again.

"How?" I was surprised.

He removed his watch and put it on the bonnet saying, "*Only one thing is constant. Time. It runs at a constant speed.*"

"Wow!" I was mesmerised by his answer, "Amazing thought."

"I have achieved all my dreams, given everything to my family, and back to the society too," he said taking out a cheque book from his blazer.

"That's great," I said looking at the pen that he took from his pocket, again a branded one. It seemed really costly, being gold plated.

"I am signing this cheque for a welfare society here for differently-abled kids," he said and signed the cheque.

"If you don't mind, can I ask something personal?"

He looked at me, straight into my eyes, smiled, "Sure! Why not! I treat you like a friend, so go ahead please."

With a lump in my throat, I took a deep breath and dared to ask, "Is there anything in life you regret?"

He paused writing the cheque. This time he didn't look at me.

"I mean," I raised my brows, "Something that you want to go back and change."

He looked at me, but his gaze was not on me. He must have been just thinking something. Honestly, I was a bit scared, so added with nervousness, "It's fine if you don't... I mean... It's Ok... sorry... I mean, I am sorry for asking this."

He looked back at the watch, rolled his thumb over the dial. But didn't say anything for as long as a minute. He was about to sign the cheque, but the next moment, he put the pen down. Then in the very next moment, he picked up the pen again and was about to sign the cheque, but stopped to think for a while. It was evident that he was struggling with something in his mind. He tried to sign, but couldn't.

He put the pen down again and took a deep breath.

"There is... something," he whispered.

"Oh!" I regretted asking that question. I might have have touched the wrong chord, I thought, and added quickly, "Are you okay? Sorry again, it's fine if you are not comfortable talking about it."

He nodded and added, "In fact, I want to speak about it."

"Okay," I whispered. I was frozen, only eyes blinking.

"Last year," he sighed and added, "It happened last year."

"Sir," I asked gathering courage, feeling his shaky voice, "Are you alright?"

"I have everything today," he continued looking at me, "You name it and I have it: money, property, time, a happy small family, but one more thing," he paused.

Silence again.

"...I have one more thing and that is the one regret," he added. "My father passed away last year."

"Oh! I am so sorry about that."

"I..." he continued with a feeble voice, "I...was...hah," he tried to smile but was unable to control his emotions. I could feel that remorse in his voice.

Still he continued, "I was so busy and engrossed in making my dreams come true that I forgot that I have parents. I was here with my small family. I gave them everything, every single moment of happiness to my kids, my wife. And likewise, I provided everything to my parents back home. I bought everything, every luxury for them. But..." he said with a lump in his throat. "But...I forgot that the way I like my kids, the way I want my kids to be with me...my parents also wanted me to be with them. I was busy making my dreams happen but I forgot that my parents had once sacrificed their dreams for my happiness."

Tears rolled down his cheeks.

"O John!" I put my hands on his shoulders and then hugged him, "You are an amazing person. You are a leader and you did the best for your family."

"Yeah, that's what I thought," he added.

"Do you need water?"

"No! You know, we used to go for holidays once a year...a new country every year. I used to visit home two or three times a year. My kids spent their vacation mostly back home, with my parents. Eventually, I got busy working here and with technology, I could order things for them online. I reduced our vacation to every other year; visits back home to once or hardly twice. My list of friends was increasing and interaction with my parents was decreasing."

I nodded to show I was listening.

"Last year, my father was hospitalised for a minor pain. I was still too busy working and decided I could visit him the next day."

"My mother told me my father wants to meet me. I promised her to fly back in the evening. In the evening I got a call that his health was not stable. I immediately got the tickets booked. During my journey, all the moments flashed in my mind that I had spent with my father; how he encouraged me, how he stood with me, how he joined me in my silly acts, how he taught me peddling the cycle, how he saved me from my mother's anger, how he told me to follow my dreams, how he made my life amazing. Right from my childhood... till now."

He took a deep breath and pulled his handkerchief out to dab out his tears. "The first thing I did after landing was to call my cousin and mother and ask them to make me talk to my father, but the doctors did not give permission due to my father's critical condition. He was being shifted to the ICU. I boarded the taxi which would take another hour to reach the hospital, so I called them up again and insisted that the doctor let me talk to him. Finally, after much effort, they agreed and my mother took the phone to my father."

His eyes filled up with tears again. "I could hear him breathing, you know. His breath was so strained and heavy, that it was audible to me even over phone. Intermittently I could hear beeps, which I assumed would be some instrument monitoring his blood pressure and pulse. I cried my heart out and said just one thing: 'I love you Dad. I love you. I am coming, I am on my way'. Then I couldn't hear him breathing anymore. All I could hear was the instrument's continuous beep deafening my ears, followed by the cries of my mother and cousins."

And then he sobbed uncontrollably. I hugged him tightly. For that moment, I also missed my parents.

"John, are you ok?" I asked as he calmed down, but he didn't reply.

"You know what," he added coughing and clearing his blocked nose and throat.

"Hmm."

"Later that day my mother told me that Dad had smiled the moment he heard my voice over phone," he said wiping his tears again.

"John!" I patted his shoulder.

He tried to smile and continued, "My Mom said that Dad was waiting only because he wanted to talk to me just one more time. That was his last wish. *Just one last time,*" he repeated and broke down into tears.

I held his hand and hugged him again. Even I couldn't help crying. Wiping off my tears I consoled him patting his back.

He continued, "I wish I could be with him that moment. I wish I could hug him. I wish I could help him getting his poems published. I wish I could express at that moment how much I loved him."

He was sobbing uncontrollably by now. "I wish I could…" he said putting his palms on his face, "O God! I wish I could."

"I want to go back and change this," he said looking at me.

And I was lost in my own thoughts.

❖

Parents need nothing but your love and care. Your dreams are necessary, but not as much as your parents. You may not realise it right now, but you need them as much as they need you. It's just that you're so caught up in things around, that you get very late in realising this.

Sometimes, think about *their* dreams too. Those that they left for your happiness. Take out some time to make their dreams come true.

This universe is an ocean of happiness where distance is measured in SPH, Smiles Per Hour.

So spread that happiness at home first, starting with your parents. Play with them all of the small games that they used to teach you in your childhood. Hug them often, take them out on a date, learn something new with them so that they get that pleasure to guide you again, so that they live their first year of parenthood again.

You need no book or a person to tell you how to make your parents happy. You know it well. Do it.

9

*Rise in love with passion,
for falling is the old fashion.*

❧

*Happiness is...rising in LOVE,
in spite of gravity.*

❖

Your best efforts for living your dreams give you immense happiness, but dreams turn great if you have someone with whom you can live these moments.

If it's just the dinner, it's about the food and place; if it's love, it's about the person you go with.

Love changes the way you look at life; it gives life a new perspective altogether. But it's essential to first learn to love yourself, only then will you be able to love others. The world seems beautiful through a lover's eyes.

Dare to propose, genuinely. Profess love that you feel for someone, but not to every other person you meet. Make the moments of life loveable and memorable with someone special.

A treasure hunt, handmade card, long drive, homemade chocolates, candle light dinner, salsa, etc., are little things that can create wonders.

But how does one understand love? Before you love someone else, you should learn to love yourself. Then only you will be able to love someone. Before making anyone feel special, you should know that you too are special and you deserve someone special.

To love unconditionally and commit selflessly is divinity.

When you find that special someone, express the feeling of love with simple words like a kiss on the forehead saying, "I am always there for you."

Love doesn't mean to possess; sometimes you have to let the love go. If that is for the happiness of the person you love, let it be.

❖

Love can create wonders; it can make the impossible possible.

Here is a sweet lovely story of true love and soulful connection. This story is about the self realisation of a person who was lost in finding the purpose of his life. All that he achieved in life was not alone, but through the love of his life, none other than his lady luck.

He was a successful person: well settled, leading a decently good life, working at a senior position in a well-known multi-national company. At an early stage in his life, he had achieved many of the goals he had set for himself. Despite all the success and money around, somewhere he felt that something was missing... something he was always passionate about.

There was no more spark and enthusiasm he felt in his monotonous life, which had become nothing more than just a time table for him. He started feeling bored eventually.

Confusion started creeping in his thoughts about what he exactly wanted from life. Getting frustrated with his routine work life, he wanted a big change, but didn't know what and how.

He was struggling with the big question, the question that few people get stuck with; "What is the purpose of my life?"

On the personal front, he had a bad experience in the past that had left him with a broken heart. After that, he could never get connected with any girl. He thought he had turned into a money minting machine.

Drowned in his thoughts to find what he was doing and why, he often seemed to be lost in his own world. One day in office, he was so lost in his day dreaming that he entered the ladies room. As soon as he realised his mistake, he rushed out. On the way out he bumped into a girl, who was rushing out from the gents' restroom.

Their eyes met. Something triggered in their hearts, as if two souls had met.

"Hi, I'm Viktor!" he said smiling, though was frozen with his hands raised in defence.

"Hello, I'm Kim!" she replied, with her hands also in the defensive position.

"New to the company?" he asked.

She nodded with a smile and he was mesmerised.

Their love story began, then and there. The chance meeting in front of the restrooms changed to a cup of coffee, and turned into weekend parties. Soon it grew into long chats, messages, calls and they found that they had different likes and dislikes. They didn't even realise how the talks turned into commitments.

Kim helped Viktor to find the purpose of his life and encouraged him to live his dreams that were long lost in the whims and fancies of his monotonous work life. Viktor fell – or say rose – in love for her so much that she was more to him than his own life. With his out of the box thoughts and caring nature, he won the hearts of her step parents and friends too.

Viktor finally proposed to her officially, that too in a way that every girl either imagines in her dreams or watches only in movies. Their relationship was growing better and finer with each day. They started cherishing every single moment for and with each other. With their understanding and adjustment, they were soon famous as the best couple in courtship among their acquaintances.

But...

Something happened that stole Kim from Viktor. It was so quick that he didn't get a chance to understand what was going on. Depression encumbered Viktor. He tried his best to connect with her, but all in vain. His life, once again, had turned into turmoil. Every moment, Viktor had just one thing in mind, fighting against all odds, "What should I do to bring back Kim?" How could he miraculously reignite the rays of life in Kim? How could the purest form of love bring Kim back to life?

Refer to the novel *Guru with Guitar* for answers to all these questions pertaining to love, the most powerful and magical phenomenon of all the emotions. It contains a hundred and eleven life-changing quotes. Eleven songs are also scripted therein, themed on various aspects of life like love, mother, coffee dates, etc. Eight poems celebrate and appreciate each day of the Valentines' week, and also love.

❖

Always listen to your heart. Above the practicality of life, above physical beauty and beyond money matters. There is just one attribute that stays life-long; and that is the real inner beauty, the dedication that never grows old and has no expiry date.

But if the love and its connection with the soul is being discussed here, how can breakup and disconnection be missed!

In case, for certain reasons, your relationship didn't work out, then take a break. Give yourself some time to come out of it. Stop living in the past. Crying over what didn't work last time is nothing but wastage of amazing moments that you could have created to know yourself better.

If you let go a true lover, it's your stupidity; if you are a true lover, it's your smartness to have moved out. Perhaps the other person did not deserve you.

Life is like a novel, divided into chapters. When you complete one, move on. Don't cling on to a sad chapter for long.

Pick a hobby to kill time or learn something new to keep yourself busy. Don't rush after anyone just because you are scared of being lonely.

Either you learn from or you are taught by the PEOPLE.

It is also very essential to have faith. Don't stop your feelings for someone just because you had a bad experience in the past. Just let it be and go with the flow. Get into a relationship when you are ready for it, not when you just want to get out of the previous relationship.

There is definitely someone who would bring the best out of you, the one who would surf the ebbs and flows as a great friend and stay with you forever. That's the true love.

Being over-practical or excessively emotional in taking the decision about a life partner is also a big no no. Be decent and a bit balanced, emotionally. In case people call you an emotional fool, then say this:

Emotional fool? Yes, I am. That's lot better than emotionally constipated machines; the so-called practical human beings.

Mistakes happen; but it's advisable to learn from them. They would have happened to you for a reason. Maybe life wants you to prepare and be aware for the next time. It would have a lesson to judge and stay away or handle yourself better in such situations in your life.

Love is not only expressed, it's experienced. If you feel it for someone, you will make him or her experience it too. If someone feels it for you, try to listen to it in your heart, because:

Silent words are heard through the eyes.

11

Life is all about…
Giveaways and Takeaways.

Wondering why the ninth rule is followed by the eleventh? That's because for all the *10 Golden Steps of Life*, here is the bonus step.

⌐⧓⌐

Life is all about
takeaways from the great people and
giveaways to the needy.

❖

So, take away as much as you can. The good learning from the deeds of good people has far-reaching results. There is a lot to learn all around us, and it's a good habit. Though the best lesson or teaching is lifelong friendship.

Alongside the takeaways, remember to cultivate the habit of giving back to those who need it the most. For this, you need not be rich or posses an excess of things you want to give. It can be a decent portion of your food, income, deeds or a helping hand to someone in a moment of need.

❖

Being a Chartered Accountant, I would like to share an interesting perspective of life through words of accounts.

One day, I was thinking about life and trying to understand it better. No one has actually been able to do that till now; nor was I. Hence, I was sitting lost. So I gave up and got back to work, the endless accounting work. One thing struck my mind immediately, while I was preparing financial statements.

What is Accounting?

The answer was; "It is the philosophy of recording business transactions based on three accounting principles."

My eyes glittered with joy, "What if life was an accounting process?"

I thought of applying the three principles of accounting to the transactions of life. An hour later, I came out of the tornado of entangled life, smiling. I was amazed at the results that I had found. I would like to share them with you here.

Basically, accounting divides all transactions into Debit and Credit. Each transaction has a debit amount and a credit as well, whereby each transaction's debit and credit side is always equal, i.e. balanced.

Now applying the same funda of accounting to life, it should be balanced. Coming to the three principles of accounting, all the business transactions called journal entries are divided into three categories, namely:

Personal, Nominal, and Real.

These entries involved give and take and are noted for the record purpose in the business books called accounts of the company or firm or individual. In the same way, life is also based on entries of give and take that are recorded somewhere, no one knows where. It can be proved here because you know it's true somewhere in the back of your mind. Because you acknowledge that since you did something at one point of time, now this is happening to you, etc.

Now let's look at the application of each principle of accounting to the transactions of life, with each category one by one:

1. Real: The first principle of accounting is based on real things. It's about the things that happen, based on just one question and that is "WHAT?"

    They say, *"Things come, things go; Money is a matter of to and fro."*

    So, the accounting rule is applied as follows:

    Debit what comes in;

    Credit what goes out.

    That is, if you get something then debit it; if you give something then credit that.

    For instance, if you buy a car by paying money, then the car comes in, the money goes out. So, in your accounting books, entry would be:

    Debit Car account (what comes in);

    Credit Money account (what goes out).

    Now, applying this principle to life in an instance where you get immense love from someone, and you give your heart to that person.

    Debit the love;

    Credit the heart.

    When someone brings love in your life, give them your heart.

2. Personal: The second principle is about persons. It's about recording the transactions entered into with people, based on just one question, which is "WHO?"

So, the rule is applied as follows:

Debit the receiver;

Credit the giver.

That is, if you receive something, debit the person who receives it and credit the one who gives.

Now imagine you buy a car on installments, then the car comes in, and the seller is the creditor.

So, in your accounting books, the entry would be:

Debit car account (what comes, Rule 1);

Credit seller's account (the giver, Rule 2).

And, in the books of the seller:

Debit buyer's account (the receiver, Rule 2);

Credit car/sales account (what goes out, Rule 1).

Now, applying it to life:

For example, if you get happiness from someone then:

The receiver of happiness is indebted. So give the credit to the giver, in form of regards.

Debit Happiness;

Credit Someone.

You get happiness when you help someone.

3. Nominal: The third principle is for recording profits and losses. It's about non-existing things that happen due to Real things, based on just one question, which is "HOW?"

So, the rule is applied as follows:

Debit the expense;

Credit the income.

That is to say, if you spend, debit it; if you earn, credit that.

Take the instance when you get a car on rent. Then, in your books, you'll write:

Debit the rent (the expense, Rule 3);

Credit the owner (the giver, Rule 2).

Now, join take to next page applying it to Life:

In case someone shows courage, that person gets respect in return.

Debit the courage;

Credit the respect.

Courage is the only currency, where the more you spend, the richer you become. By earning respect.

❖

Further, for all Chartered Accountants in the world, I would like to devote a few quotes to appreciate and motivate the professionals and their services to the society and fraternity.

These quotes would be helpful especially for those who get disheartened due to challenges of life or failures in the exams. These quotes would not only make these students cherish their victory (for those who clear the exams), but also motivate (those who fail) so as not to give up their dreams.

Before going ahead, I have a message for those who tried to become members of the fraternity, and could not.

Don't treat yourself as if you have failed. Take it as a challenge and come up with more enthusiasm and a robust study plan; because:

A room full of success has doors called failures.

Don't get disheartened. I too had failed in Chartered Accountancy. I am happy today as I chose to reappear and completed my dream of becoming a CA. Don't listen to people who say you can't do it.

If people tell you that you can't do it, then it actually means that they can't do it.

Prove them wrong by re-appearing and becoming a CA or taking to the finish line any other study course that you are pursuing. It's your dream and you have to toil to achieve it. Plan well, revise well and you'll be able to crack it.

Here are the ten quotes especially written for Chartered Accountants and aspirants. Read these and feel the energy inside, then use it positively to fly high. Come on, give it a try!

1. From the balance sheet of humanity, to the profit and loss account of emotions, I am in all the good books. I am a Chartered Accountant.

2. Happiness is starting your study with 3 principles of accounting; then going into your profession with 3 principles of life: challenge it, achieve it, loop it. I am a Chartered Accountant.

3. CA means Can-do Attitude. I may fail, but I would not give up, because I believe I can. I am a Chartered Accountant.

4. CA means Chakra of Ambitions. I am a Chartered Accountant.

5. CA means Charismatic Amalgamation of great experiences of life. I am a Chartered Accountant.

6. CA means Challenge it, Achieve it, Loop it. I am a Chartered Accountant.

7. Challenges Ahead? Huh! Who cares! I am a CA, Chartered Accountant.

8. CA study course in India is not the toughest study course. It's for them who are the toughest, the determined ones. I am a Chartered Accountant.

9. Someone asked, "Can anybody...?" A CA replied, "Yes, and I don't think I just can, I know I will. I am a Chartered Accountant."

And the last one is especially for CA students:

10. A CA student is a composition of a compassionate, cheerful, and cool aspirant. I will be a Chartered Accountant.

❖

Now a few tips on preparation for exams:

1. Knowing your weakness is the first step towards success.

Check the root cause of your fears of failure. It can be one or both of the following:
- Punctuality / lack of time management; and/or
- Divided concentration / attention.

Time flies at the speed of light during the preparatory days. Check if you are not able to give ample time for studies to individual subjects or whether it's the concentration that gets disrupted when you sit to study.

2. Making your weakness your strength is the second step towards success.

Win your fears and mould these into your strengths. The problems identified can be solved by the following tricks:
- Make a time table and follow it strictly;
- Find innovative ways to enhance concentration.

Making a time table is the toughest job for some students. Here is a golden tip for how to create a time table. Suppose you want to study 8 subjects in 3 months of preparatory days, i.e. you have 90 days to prepare and revise.

Calculation is simple:
- 8 days for each subject for first revision.
- 2 days for each subject for second revision.

It comes out to be 80 days in total for all the 8 subjects and you still have 10 days of reserve. Give them to the toughest subject, like 2 days for 4 toughest subjects. Woohoo, you are still left with 2 reserve days.

Now, allocate time the way you want. Use two methods. Either use the horizontal method, i.e. complete 1 subject in 8 days in one go or use the vertical method, i.e. give 2 hours for 1 subject covering all 8 subjects simultaneously every 2 days.

To check your progress, divide the number of pages of the book of one subject with the available hours. For instance, if a book of income tax has 400 pages in total, then divide them by 8 days. Which means you'll have to cover 50 pages per day. Sometimes you would cover 50 pages in 10 hours and sometimes in 4 hours. It depends on the type of subject, if it's practical one with numerical or theoretical one with narratives.

To enhance concentration, take breaks. Watch 30 minutes of stand-up comedy during meals or listen to songs. If one subject is boring for you, then use vertical method as stated above, i.e. studying two subjects simultaneously.

Drink loads of water so that you have to get up every 1 hour for the bio-break. It'll keep you healthy and fresh. Also include the ergonomics as to posture, place to study, healthy food habits, etc.

3.   Talk to yourself, boot-up yourself.

No one else can understand you better than you yourself. So talk to yourself once a day; sometimes quietly and sometimes aloud. Tell yourself, "I can and I will do it."

Believe me. It works! This way you'll guide your subconscious mind to go get things you dream of. If possible, put a printout on the study table and ceiling with these words so you keep seeing it and feel motivated.

4. Homework. Do it before you go to the classroom.

Prepare, not quantitatively, but qualitatively. Your homework will strengthen your confidence. Similarly, for your exams, be prepared. Make sure you have studied the subject once in detail and have already done two types of revisions stated above, i.e. firstly eight days per subject and secondly two days of quick revision per subject.

5. Prioritise. Prefer Today and Tomorrow to Yesterday.

Anything that is to be done today should be done today only. Do it on priority; leave everything else till tomorrow. If there's anything you lost, that was yesterday. Let it go. Concentrate on today.

Plan your tomorrow today, learning from yesterday.

During exams, if you think you are not going as per the time table and you have wasted let's say one month and now left with just two months to revise. *Do not* worry. There is still time.

6. Defrag and Rearrange.

Once in a week, rearrange all your things, be it planner, time table, cupboard, books, kitchen, office... anything. In the same way, rearrange your mind too, by cultivating a hobby. Take time off, play guitar, go dance, read books, do anything you like.

During exams, give time to your hobby. Let's say about ten minutes after every four odd hours. Do watch comedy videos and do listen to songs. You'll feel rejuvenated. But don't spend more time on these hobbies, a short break only.

7. Learn the ABC of things.

To nail a peg, learn WHAT size of hammer is required and WHY. Learn the ABC or theory or logic of things that you want to master. Lighter hammer on a bigger nail and vice-versa - both result in failure.

Same applies to exams as well. Learn the logic of the formula being applied; don't cram. If anyhow you can't remember the topic without cramming, then learn the sequence in innovative ways. Like SMARTU can be the acronym for learning characteristics of a topic that goes as - Symmetric, Multiple functioning, Applicability, Resources, Timeliness and Uniformity.

8.   Laugh at life before life laughs at you.

Learn to laugh aloud. You should not worry in two cases: one, when you have control over the situation; two, when you can't control it. So whenever you fail, first laugh, then do the postmortem on why you failed. Learn to laugh at life, not yourself.

During exams, don't cry over subjects you don't like to study. There's no other choice; you have to master it.

9.   Keep toiling the mill of your mind yourself; leave no room for the devil to tame the idleness of your mind.

Don't sit idle. Do it yourself, for no one else will do it for you. Take the charge of your life and never be free to waste even a single minute doing nothing, till you achieve your goal. After that, you won't ever feel like sitting idle doing nothing.

So give your best in the preparation. The hard work repays, sometimes in terms of satisfaction and sometimes in the form of bills. Keep yourself so busy with studies and small breaks that the devil should get no time to disrupt your thoughts.

10. They *are the victorious who dare not to give up.*

Never ever give up. Even if you fail every time, give it one more try. Make a log of your progress. Put ticks on the calendar. If you fall short of time, sleep seven hours instead of eight. Believe me, you won't regret it once you clear your exams.

Don't even think of giving up, neither your ambitions, nor a single topic of any subject. Make a single minded goal of becoming what you want to be and you'll realise it.

❖

All the rules stated here are tried and tested.*

*Conditions apply ;)

Disclaimer: By applying all the rules mentioned in this book, it's not sure that you get desired results. But one thing that you would get for sure is satisfaction; if not immediate, it might take years, decades, ages, but you will have *no regrets*.

Cheers.

10

Start NOW…
for it expires second by second.

✤

The best day to start anything is
TODAY;
and the best time,
NOW.

❖

"One day I shall…" is the most loved dialogue of those who find excuses rather than the right time to start something.

The problem with time is that it never comes back.

Life is short; make the best of it. Greatest wastes are those people whose hobby is to sit idle and do nothing. Don't be in that group.

Take that first tiny step. Make a blue print at least. Once you do that, you will feel the urge to start working on it.

❖

To know the importance of starting something that you always wanted to, this story is a perfect fit.

There was a person who always wanted to write a great novel. He knew what to write and how to execute the plan, but didn't know when to start.

He missed his home country whenever he used to fly for long term official assignments abroad. More than that, he always struggled to find time to sit and write his dream novel.

Once he was in a plane, going on one of the most amazing assignments that he had been asking his manager to put him on. It was an hour before the landing. Getting bored of reading and sleeping from the past five hours on the plane, he quickly pulled out a paper from his pocket and started writing.

Hardly had he written two lines after brainstorming when he felt a jerk. Ignoring that, he looked outside the window, but it was dark. He thought himself to be stuck in that situation, the moment of darkness, when he didn't know what to write.

Curling his lips as he looked at the dim-lit seat belt signal, another jerk was felt; this time a stronger one.

"Is this plane going to crash?" he smirked. Next moment his eyes glittered, with a smile he wrote the title "*Living beyond life.*" As he was underlining it, another strong jerk jolted the plane.

The seat belt signals were turned on. Looking around at other passengers, he held the paper tight. The turbulence increased and all the passengers seemed visibly scared. Another strong jolt and a lady passenger shrieked.

"Your attention please," the pilot announced, "We are going through bad weather, please fasten your seat belts."

He was tense now. He looked at the paper he was writing on, quickly folded that up, fastened his seatbelt and held the seat armrests tightly.

Turbulence was increasing by the second. "Crew! Please take your seats," announced the pilot and the airhostesses ran towards their seats. The jolts were getting stronger.

With another strong jolt, exit signs were lit up. All the couples, kids, grownups and elderly people in the plane were badly scared; so was he. An elderly couple experienced difficulty in breathing. A nearby passenger quickly pulled down the oxygen masks for them and helped them wear it.

A lady sitting behind shrieked again as they felt another jolt. He looked back, and was more scared to see her holding an infant who was asleep.

"Oh God!" he murmured with the next thunder, tightened his grip over the armrest and pushed his head on the headrest, closing his eyes tightly.

As the wobbling increased, passengers screamed; so did he, opening his eyes. He looked around, all scared faces, with the fear of death written all over. He too was afraid to die, but he started talking to himself, "Oh God! I should not die today. I should not die. I have so much to do. God please! I should not die."

He closed his eyes tight again and started murmuring, "One more chance. God please! One chance. I don't want to die. At least not *now*. Please."

With every twitch, his heartbeat was increasing and shrieks of other passengers too. But he was just busy talking to himself. In fact, he was shouting aloud, with eyes shut tight, "I want to tell my Mom and Dad I love them so much. I want to meet Kim, my love, and hug her once. I want to meet my bestie once. Please! God! I want to say sorry to the ones I have hurt ever. God! I want to live my dreams. I want to become an author. I want to write. Please, give me one chance. Please, I will..."

As he was about to complete, the turbulence reduced.

"I will..." he repeated, shouting.

And there was total silence.

He opened his one eye and found that everyone was looking at him. He opened the second one, gave a weird smiled to people around. Then he turned to the passenger next to him and said sheepishly, "I want to become an author."

The passenger sitting next to him was in his sixties, nodded, "Yes my son. Relax. Everything is under control now."

The plane was on a smooth run and the passengers seemed a bit relaxed. They hugged their families, couples kissed.

He had tears rolling down his cheeks, just like various other passengers. The difference was that, by chance, he was the only one in that flight who had no one known to wipe off his tears.

"We have crossed the bad weather," announced the pilot, "Please remain seated with your seat belts on till further announcements, and please stay calm."

It was a miraculous save, another life. The only difference was that he seemed to have realised the real value of life.

After reaching the hotel he called up his parents back home though it was late night there. "I am missing you both a lot," he said and started sobbing.

"Aww! My baby," his mother consoled him. "What happed to my brave son?" They talked for another hour remembering the silly things he did in childhood and he slept peacefully.

He wrote all the feelings that he had experienced throughout the plane journey that proved to be the life changing lesson for him and he sent it to the editor of a national newspaper.

Next morning, his mother called him up and the first thing she said was, "I love you my son and I know you love us a lot." She started sobbing.

"Aww! My mommy," he mimicked her. "What happened to my brave mommy?"

"Your article is published in the newspaper," she replied.

He had tears of joy realising that the time had come to live his dreams now.

❖

They, who turn their aspirations into actions, achieve their dreams.

The difference between a signature and an autograph is that the second one has higher face value on a plain paper than the first one even on a cheque.

To make that happen, the first thing is to pick your pen and write that first letter of your signature.

There is no such phenomenon called 'the right time' because time is always right; it's the thoughts, situations or the people that are wrong or dubious.

The earlier you realise, the better you start off. Don't over-think.

Stop procrastinating. Stop delaying things. Stop telling yourself that you'll be taking that first step tomorrow.

The biggest regret a few years down the line would be...I wish I could. So dare to do what you dream of...NOW.

The best way to kill procrastination is to give your two minutes to the task. Don't wait, don't think much. If you want to start living your dreams, just start right away.

The world changes with that one tiny step. Dare it NOW.

❖